› FROM
ENDO WAR
TO
INNER PEACE

My Healing Journey from
Stage IV Endometriosis

WENKE LANGHOF

BALBOA.PRESS
A DIVISION OF HAY HOUSE

Copyright © 2025 Wenke Langhof.

All rights reserved. No part of this book may be used or reproduced by any means, graphic, electronic, or mechanical, including photocopying, recording, taping or by any information storage retrieval system without the written permission of the author except in the case of brief quotations embodied in critical articles and reviews.

Balboa Press books may be ordered through booksellers or by contacting:

Balboa Press
A Division of Hay House
1663 Liberty Drive
Bloomington, IN 47403
www.balboapress.co.uk
UK TFN: 0800 0148647 (Toll Free inside the UK)
UK Local: (02) 0369 56325 (+44 20 3695 6325 from outside the UK)

Because of the dynamic nature of the Internet, any web addresses or links contained in this book may have changed since publication and may no longer be valid. The views expressed in this work are solely those of the author and do not necessarily reflect the views of the publisher, and the publisher hereby disclaims any responsibility for them.

The author of this book does not dispense medical advice or prescribe the use of any technique as a form of treatment for physical, emotional, or medical problems without the advice of a physician, either directly or indirectly. The intent of the author is only to offer information of a general nature to help you in your quest for emotional and spiritual well-being. In the event you use any of the information in this book for yourself, which is your constitutional right, the author and the publisher assume no responsibility for your actions.

Any people depicted in stock imagery provided by Getty Images are models, and such images are being used for illustrative purposes only. Certain stock imagery © Getty Images.

Interior Graphics/Art Credit: Nina Rae
Cover image/Art Credit: Laura Naughton

Print information available on the last page.

ISBN: 978-1-9822-8934-8 (sc)
ISBN: 978-1-9822-8935-5 (e)

Balboa Press rev. date: 02/10/2025

DEDICATED TO BUSTER

Thank you for being by my side throughout
my biggest pain and biggest growth.
Thank you for cuddling up to me, when I allowed
the tears to fall, unseen by human eyes. Thank you
for making me go out in nature twice every day:
nature is where I recharge my batteries and regain my strength.
Thank you for teaching me how to live in the
moment and enjoy the little things.
Thank you for your truly unconditional love.
I couldn't have done it without you!

Buster 2009-2023

DISCLAIMER

Any information given in this book is to be taken solely as advisory in nature. Wenke Langhof will not be held personally, legally, or financially liable for any action taken based upon their advise. Wenke Langhof is not a psychologist or medical professional and is unable to diagnose, prescribe, treat, or cure any ailment. Anyone using the information in this book acknowledges that they have read and understand the details of this disclaimer. The principle ideas and actions discussed in this book are based on Wenke's own experience. By utilizing and using this book, the participant acknowledges that s/he assumes full responsibility for the knowledge gained herein and its application. Material in this book is not intended to replace the advice of a competent healthcare practitioner. The reader takes full responsibility for the way they utilize and exercise the information in this book.

CONTENTS

Acknowledgements xi
Prologue xv

Part 1 Illness

Chapter 1   A Normal Period Night 1
Chapter 2   Finally! An Official Diagnosis 5
Chapter 3   A Holiday from Endometriosis 13
Chapter 4   Different Countries, Different Ways 20
Chapter 5   Being Silenced - Losing My Voice 32
Chapter 6   Dark Night of the Soul 39

Part 2 Healing

Chapter 7   Reiki – My First Step to Inner Peace 47
Chapter 8   The Tempest 53
Chapter 9   A New Door Opens 58
Chapter 10   Decision Time: Surgery or Germany 62
Chapter 11   The 3E Centre 69
Chapter 12   Assessment Week 73
Chapter 13   The Warburg Effect & Budwig's Findings 78
Chapter 14   Embracing a Budwig Day 84
Chapter 15   Awareness Is Rising 89
Chapter 16   Listening to My Needs 95
Chapter 17   Gratitude and Stillness 97
Chapter 18   Laughter and Happiness 100

Chapter 19	The Language of Our Body	102
Chapter 20	My Grandmother's Story	108
Chapter 21	Passed on Trauma - Healing My Ancestry Line	118
Chapter 22	A Day of Silence	128
Chapter 23	Emotions as Energy	136
Chapter 24	Returning Home	139
Chapter 25	Sticking to My Guns	144
Chapter 26	Healed Naturally	150

Epilogue 155
Appendix 1 Endometriosis - A Subconscious Fear of
     Pregnancy 165
Appendix 2 Fight or Flight - The Human Stress Response 171
Appendix 3 Healing the Divine Feminine 175
Glossary A-Z 179
Bibliography & Further Reading 185

ACKNOWLEDGEMENTS

Everything recounted in this book is my own, individual, personal experience. My mum once said to me, if you put ten people in a room and let them all experience the same thing, you will end up with ten different stories. What makes up our life is not what happened to us, but what meaning we give it. What's the story we tell ourselves? What's the narrative we chose to hang on to?

What I learned on my journey is that we can change the narrative, chose a different story and free ourselves of the past. I am not here to tell anyone what they should or shouldn't do. I am simply here to share my story, one story of currently 8 billion individual and unique human stories being lived on this planet we call Earth.

Writing my story down has helped me immensely to process my journey and this in itself has been very healing. Looking back at the younger version of me you'll meet in this book, I realise just how far I've come, how much I have changed and how proud I am of what I have achieved – often against all odds. For a long time, it felt like an uphill struggle. In hindsight, every single push, every step, every obstacle was needed and I carry so much gratitude for all of it.

'If it doesn't kill you, it makes you strong,' my mother used to say. How true she was! I thank my family and friends for their patience, and for staying right by my side while I changed, while I worked things out for myself, while I needed space to retreat, while I burned old versions of myself and carefully crafted new ones, only to burn them as well and carry on shaping and forming, constantly evolving. Thank you all for not deserting me, but for hanging in there and adjusting to all those different versions, for trusting me and often changing yourselves in the process.

I hope that my story will give hope to the millions of women suffering from endometriosis. The millions of women who are being told that they just have to live with this debilitating disease, or that hysterectomies are the solution they seek, when they are at best a short term fix with irreversible consequences that may far outweigh the benefits gained, at least for some. Based on my own experience, I believe, endometriosis is a lifestyle illness and, like most chronic illnesses, can be managed and healed by lifestyle changes. Enjoy my story, but be aware that we are all unique and it is down to you to write your own story.

Thank you to all those that have helped me put these words to paper. You know who you are and I deeply love and cherish having you in my life. Your input has been invaluable in transforming my first manuscript into the book you now hold in your hand. Thank you Nina Rae for the illustrations, I personally love how you created an endo warrior in slippers and my absolute favourite is the immune policeman on holiday. Thank you Laura Naughton for creating the beautiful book cover image specially for me.

All names and place names have been either omitted completely or changed to protect the identities and privacy of people involved. Even my own name is different to the name I go by in everyday life. Growing up, Emmie was my nickname. It was only used by my family and most often when I had done something that they regarded as silly, when I had made a mistake or expressed ideas that were a bit mad in my family's eyes. Imagine an exacerbated "Oh, Emmie!" I loved having a nickname, so using Emmie in this story just feels right.

I am grateful for all the doctors and healthcare professionals that were part of my journey. I believe, the universe always gives you what's right for you at any given time. I needed to learn to stand in my own truth, and in order to do that, I needed people who challenged that truth. I do not judge anyone, we are all here playing the roles we were given by life. We all do the best we can at any given time with the knowledge we have. I have met many healthcare professionals in my life, and I would say by far the vast majority (maybe even all of them) had a true desire to help people heal. I personally don't think, however, that the healthcare systems we currently have, always provide the best conditions needed for true healing.

The changes we so desperately need in this world will start in each one of us. My world changed when I finally stopped looking for solutions to my problems outside of me, and started to turn inwards. It's when I started exploring myself, my beliefs and my desires, that healing started to happen. What I learned is that we can't ever change other people. What each of us can do, 100%, without a doubt, is change ourselves. Who we are is the only thing we have total control over. And if who you currently are is not who you want to be, then you can change that version of you. Upgrade.

I do wish with all my heart that this book becomes an inspiration to those who read it, like so many other personal stories I have read were an inspiration to me. May it bring hope to those suffering from endometriosis and other chronic illnesses, and may it show that there is always a light at the end of the tunnel, that healing is indeed possible.

The road of life is full of bends and twists, ups and downs. We can sit and wait our whole life for the road ahead to be made perfect, we can rage at all the potholes, or we can embrace the unknown and go on the best adventure any of us can ever go on: the journey of finding ourselves. This is my journey. I hope you enjoy reading it.

Lots of love,
Wenke

PROLOGUE

"In my spare time I like reading. I'm especially keen on reading about experiences of other people overcoming serious diseases."
(Wenke, 1995, Au pair application at age 18)

"When I get home, I shall write a book about this place."
(Lewis Carroll, 1865, Alice in Wonderland)

"Make sure you write about something you have experienced yourself, because then you will write with authenticity."
(Stranger on a plane, 2017)

PART ONE
ILLNESS

"When pain, misery, or anger happen, it is time to look within you, not around you. To achieve well-being the only one who needs to be fixed is *you*." (Sadhguru: Inner Engineering - A Yogi's Guide to Joy. Penguin Random House India, 2016)

CHAPTER 1
A NORMAL PERIOD NIGHT

I am kneeling on the oak stained timber planks of my bathroom floor, rocking back and forth, waiting for the wave of pain to wash over me. I scream as loud as I can inside my head. A silent scream, so I don't wake my husband David. I cry unheard tears, bound in unwitnessed pain. I sob, my chest heaving up and down with pure desperation. My hands are pressing down on my mouth, muffling the tiny noise that occasionally manages to escape my lips, despite my attempts at suffering in silence. I swear, yet the words remain locked in my throat. I feel totally empty, staring into nothingness, wishing I wasn't here anymore. I am cold and numb. Slowly, I crawl back into bed: shivering, exhausted. I fall asleep for just another hour before it's time to get up and face the day.

Hello day! My main aim today? Holding it together. Don't let anyone see how I really feel. I can do this! I've done it so many times before. Smile. Let's go! Empty the dishwasher. Porridge for my husband, scrambled eggs for my son, quick cuddle for the dog, refill the water bottles, turn the washing machine on. "Quick, put your shoes on, darling. Time to go!" Ushering my son out of the front door. "Have a lovely day," I sing high pitched to my husband as I throw him an air kiss. Does he notice, the joyous tone in my voice is fake? School drop off. Walk the dog. Feed the dog. Put washing in the dryer. Tidy. Hoover.

Prepare lessons. I'm a language tutor. Can I cancel today's lesson? I'm really not feeling well. Take paracetamol. Drive to client to teach business German. Shift my tender bottom from left to right on the office chair. Smile. The paracetamol is wearing off. I can just about get to the end of the lesson. Deep breath in the car. Collect the last bit of strength to focus on the drive home. Can't take another painkiller yet, it's too early says the medical leaflet. School pick up. God, I'm exhausted. Cook dinner. Read my son a bedtime story. Bath. Finally, the salvation of another painkiller. Hot water bottle. Bed. That's a good period day.

A bad period day is spent on the sofa. Writhing and not knowing how to position any part of my body so the pain becomes bearable, and wishing with my whole heart I would just pass out. My mind wonders back to East German school assemblies. One of my friends used to pass out regularly, standing in line in the school yard. I did sometimes envy her ability to pass out at those boring gatherings that seemed to go on forever. Why can't I pass out? In movies people always pass out when the pain gets too much. Is this level of pain not enough yet?

I really cannot imagine bearing any more pain. This is what childbirth must be like. I had my son Jack by caesarean. There is a tiny part of me that feels a little guilty for having had placenta previa, which allowed me to avoid the pain of giving birth to a new life. I always feel like I'm not quite a proper mother, because of it.

Is my monthly endometriosis pain pay back for the joy I felt, when the maternity nurse told me I would need a caesarean? "You're only at 20 weeks, the placenta may still move to the side in your third trimester. Don't worry, you may still be able to give birth naturally," she encouraged me, her voice full of empathy, pity and hope. She clearly felt pushing a melon through my vagina was the preferable choice of bringing a new soul into the world. I prayed to God to just leave that placenta exactly where it was. I was scared of the pain.

Now I am in pain every month, every moon cycle, every period. It's not just the pain in my lower abdomen. I can't wee, I am desperate to go to the toilet, but nothing comes out. However hard I try to squeeze, there seems to be no communicative connection between my brain and the muscles responsible for opening the bladder tract. I stick my finger into my vagina trying to massage what I figure must be the exit route through which that urine pipe must run, resulting in a little oh so welcome trickle running down my hand. A tiny bit of relief at last. Even though it doesn't last long, it is pure bliss. I know my bladder is still full. Sometimes I strip off and jump in the shower. Standing upright under running water helps to release the blocked flow. I remember the boys once on a skiing trip discussing who did or didn't wee in the shower, their opinions ranging from 'doesn't everyone' to 'how disgusting'. I kept very quiet during that conversation!

Number twos are equally troublesome. I have spent my life being constipated. This was a dream for my mum, who used to proudly tell me that even as a baby I never produced a dirty nappy. Instead I would poop cute little rabbit pellets onto a piece of tissue paper neatly positioned under my cute little bum while she changed my nappy. What a dream child! Much better than my naughty brother who would fill the whole nappy full of poo that ended up running up his whole backside, oozing out of the sides. Not like clean, perfect, constipated, little me. No, no, no! Growing up, being constipated was my normal. In fact, with my mum lovingly telling that story, I was almost proud of never having had a proper shit.

I am in agony. It feels like I can't push anything out. The muscles responsible for moving my stool down and out seem to have stopped functioning. The pain is horrendous. On top of the normal period pain I have the worst stomach ache you can imagine. Having a good old shit would solve at least part of my problems, but the exit gate remains shut and whoever has got the key has gone. It actually feels like it's all piling up behind the gate, but the anus muscles are totally unresponsive. I put Vaseline on my finger and reach inside my bum hole. I manage to scrape out some little pellets of poo, but not enough to truly cause relief.

I speak to my gynaecologist about the constipation and she tells me to get glycerine tablets and just take laxatives regularly. I can't see how that can be a healthy long-term solution. Nevertheless, I do get some herbal laxatives, they don't do much though. The constipation and pain are worse on the first two days of my period, so I decide just not to eat on those two days. I never feel like eating anything anyway when the pain is really bad, and I am sure my body can survive a couple of days of fasting. I eat a little watery porridge or flaxseeds soaked in water. This usually helps smoothen the bowel passage. My monthly cycle continues. I feel trapped being a woman.

CHAPTER 2
FINALLY! AN OFFICIAL DIAGNOSIS

"… Much… much… worse… than… we… thought…," I hear the doctor say. It is a day in January 2011. I drift in and out of that lovely cotton wool cloud that exists between a general anaesthetic and the real world. Opening my eyes seems such an effort, whereas letting myself fall back into that white oblivion is absolute bliss. Something is pulling me back though. Someone is calling my name. I open my eyes and smile. The smile is automatic. What I'm smiling at is my surgeon's face. She is sitting on a chair at the foot of my bed and I think she wants to go home. She also smiles a smile she doesn't want to smile, by the looks of it. She is talking to me. I see her lips move, but I can't hear a thing. I reach back into the white cloud to grab my conscious mind and force myself back into the body that is lying on the hospital bed. My body. The body that has just had a laparoscopy[1].

"I haven't been able to do anything. Everything in there was too red and angry to laser. We need to get the inflammation down first. I'll arrange for you to come and see me in two weeks to discuss your options."

Much worse than we thought. Much worse than we thought. Much worse than we thought. Haven't been able to do anything. Haven't been able to do anything. Not done anything. Much worse. Much worse. Tears well up. My throat is tight. Inside my world is falling apart, but I can still feel that stupid smile on my face. Am I dying? Have I got cancer? No I'm pretty sure she didn't

---
[1] See list of medical terms at the end of this chapter or use the Glossary A-Z at the end of the book.

say cancer. Oh God! Why did I not listen? What have I got? I can't speak. A ball of fear is blocking my throat.

> "Are you ok?"
> "Fine," I croak.
> "Don't worry. Recover and I will see you in two weeks. You'll be fine," and off she goes.

34 years old, laparoscopy, and now I have to wait for two weeks to find out what is wrong with me. All I know is that whatever it is, I have got is much worse than we thought. Bloody hell. Stupid anaesthetic. Why didn't I listen!? I'm so exhausted.

A few hours later, my husband comes to pick me up. That's the good thing about private healthcare. They want the bed, so you're out quickly. He wants to know what the surgeon said and the tears well up again, but I push them back down before he can notice. My husband lost his first wife to breast cancer. Big smile, "They haven't been able to do anything, as everything was really inflamed. I'll see the consultant in two weeks to discuss my options. In the meantime, we'll have to wait for her letter, as I have no idea what she said I had. But it wasn't cancer." Big smile again… a long out-breath. Whatever we get diagnosed with these days seems to be ok as long as it's not cancer. Cancer kills. Everything else is fine. You live.

The letter from my consultant arrives a week later. It's the one they send to your general practitioner and you get copied in, so it's full of medical terms I've never heard of. Apparently, I have stage IV endometriosis on my uterus, ovaries and colon and extensive endometriosis in the pouch of Douglas.

I quite like that I have a 'Pouch of Douglas', it sounds interesting and adventurous, a rough Scottish Douglas fir wilderness hiding inside me. I also have ovarian endometriomas, a retroflexed uterus and fibrosis. I have to google most of these words and make a mental note of starting my own dictionary of medical terms. I feel a bit lost reading about my health in what feels like a foreign language. Actually, it is a foreign language in a foreign language, as I am German. English is not my mother tongue, but after almost two decades of living in this country, it has become the language I think and dream in. It looks like I now have to learn another language: medical English.

Google teaches me that endometriosis is a chronic illness, where cells that are normally found in the womb, for some unknown reason, appear outside of the womb and inside the abdomen. I imagine a layer of cling-film-like cells that attach themselves where they shouldn't be. What's the big deal? The big deal comes once a month, when my body releases little messenger hormones that tell the cells which form the lining of my womb, that no fertilized egg has been implanted and that their services – to form a cosy nest of blood supply for a baby – are not required this month and my period starts.

Those little messenger hormones are programmed to speak to all the cells that form the endometrium. Just as if they were inside the womb, the cells that have escaped my womb and cling to my ovaries and my colon get the message and dutifully start to bleed. The trouble is, there is no outlet: no cervix, no vagina, no exit route. I effectively bleed internally and the blood has nowhere to go. The bleeding cells are stuck to my organs, which naturally don't like having something stuck to them. So they start reacting with inflammation to tell the immune cells to come and sort out whatever is going on.

The immune cells are ace. Like policemen on duty they arrive and sort things out. The trouble is, that this happens every month and those police guys have lots of other jobs to do as well. After months and months of this, they're overworked and it takes them longer and longer to sort out the inflammation. My body is trying to make me aware of the inflammation and sends signals to my brain; the message I receive is encoded as pain. The more fed up my organs get, the more pain I feel. Basically everyone - me, my organs, my body, my immune cells - is tired, exhausted and fed up, ready for a holiday.

I search online for descriptions of endometriosis pain. What comes up are phrases like 'hundreds of knives slashing your insides', 'your insides being ripped apart', 'electrical shocks ripping through you'. As I'm ploughing through the internet pages, I come across a picture an artist suffering from endo had painted. It shows a wreath of thorns round a woman's belly, oozing with blood and red inflammation. It captures exactly how I feel every month. At best, the pain is a dull ache in my abdomen, legs and buttocks that is always there, a constant companion lurking in the background of my self-awareness. At worst, it's a torture chamber I cannot escape from. I often imagine it like a dragon spewing fire inside my abdomen. At least the dragon burning me from within has finally got a name: Endometriosis, or endo for short.

When I finally see my consultant gynaecologist again, she explains that before we can deal with the extensive endometriosis, we need to urgently get the inflammation down. She has a way of giving me, my immune cells and my tired body the holiday we so yearn for and it's called GnRH injections, trade name Prostap. For six months, we can stop those little messenger hormones that are telling my cells to bleed, by injecting male hormones that shut down my ovaries and my whole reproductive system. The injections will put me into premature menopause at the age of 34. From a hormonal point of view, I will become a man. Fabulous! I'm hoping I won't have to hoover and cook anymore either. Six whole months without periods: I've won the lottery!

I am less ecstatic when my gynaecologist explains my options after the six months: a full or partial hysterectomy (which means taking the womb and possibly ovaries out) and a less likely but possible bowel resection (removing part of my bowel). I decide to just push these thoughts aside for the moment. Let's take this bridge when we come to it. For now, I am going to make the most of six months of holiday from being a woman. No periods, yippee!

Who am I? My name doesn't really matter, for you could substitute it for millions of other names. Statistically, I am one in ten women suffering from endometriosis. But as we'll be spending the next few hours, days or weeks together – depending on how fast a reader you are – you can call me Emmie.

List of Key Medical Terms

Laparoscopy: Laparoscopy is a type of keyhole surgery used to diagnose and treat conditions. It allows a surgeon to use only small cuts and a camera for procedures inside the tummy or pelvis.
(https://www.nhs.uk/conditions/laparoscopy/)

Endometriosis: Endometriosis is where cells similar to those in the lining of the womb (uterus) grow in other parts of the body. Endometriosis usually grows in areas around the womb, such as the ovaries and fallopian tubes. It can also affect organs such as the bladder and bowel.
(https://www.nhs.uk/conditions/endometriosis/)

Uterus: The uterus or womb is the organ in the reproductive system of women that accommodates the embryonic or fetal development of one or more fertilized eggs until birth.
(https://en.wikipedia.org/wiki/Uterus)

Retroflexed uterus: A retroverted (or retroflexed) uterus is a common condition that describes how your uterus sits within your pelvis. A retroverted, or tilted, uterus is when your uterus is tilted backward toward your spine. It doesn't cause any serious health problems but can cause discomfort during sex and painful menstruation.
(https://my.clevelandclinic.org/health/diseases/23426-retroverted-uterus)

Pouch of Douglas: The pouch of Douglas (rectovaginal pouch, or cul-de-sac) is the extension of the peritoneum into the space between the back wall of the womb and the rectum in the human female.
(https://en.wikipedia.org/wiki/Rectouterine_pouch) [Author's note: it's a tiny empty space between the womb and the anus.]

Endometrioma: Endometriomas are usually benign growths, most often found in the ovary, often called chocolate cysts. They form dark fluid filled cysts, which can vary greatly in size. The fluid inside the cyst is thick, dark, old blood, giving it a chocolate-like appearance.
(https://en.wikipedia.org/wiki/Emdometrioma)

Ovary: The ovary (from Latin *ovarium* or egg, nut) is a gonad in the female reproductive system that produces eggs. When released, an egg travels from the ovaries through the fallobian tubes into the uterus. There is an ovary on the left and right side of the body. The ovaries are endocrine glands, secreting various hormones that play an important role in the female menstrual cycle and fertility.
(http://en.wikipedia.org/wiki/Ovary)

Ovarian: relating to the ovaries (see above)

Fibrosis is also known as scarring. It is uncontrolled wound healing in which connective tissue replaces normal parenchymal tissue to the extent that it goes unchecked, leading to considerable tissue remodelling and the formation of permanent scar tissue. Repeated injuries, chronic inflammation and repair are susceptible to fibrosis.
(https://en.wikipedia.org/wiki/Fibrosis#:~:text=Fibrosis%2C%20also%20known%20as%20fibrotic,formation%20of%20permanent%20scar%20tissue)

Womb: see uterus above

Cervix: The cervix is a small canal that connects the uterus and vagina. It allows fluids to leave and enter the uterus. During childbirth, the cervix widens so that a baby can be born.
(https://my.clevelandclinic.org/health/body/23279-cervix)

Vagina: The vagina is the elastic, muscular reproductive organ of the female genital tract. It extends from the vulva to the cervix.
(https://en.wikipedia.org/wiki/Vagina)

GnRH (Prostap): Stands for gonadotropin-releasing hormone and is involved in making the male and female sex hormones testosterone, estrogen and progesterone.
(https://my.clevelandclinic.org/health/body/22525-gonadotropin-releasing-hormone). Prostap is simply the brand name of a chemically produced version of these hormones.

> **Hysterectomy**: A hysterectomy is the surgical procedure to remove the womb from a woman's body.
> (https://www.nhs.uk/conditions/hysterectomy/)
>
> **Bowel resection:** A bowel resection is a surgery to remove any part of the bowel.
> (https://www.webmd.com/colorectal-cancer/bowel-resection)

CHAPTER 3
A HOLIDAY FROM ENDOMETRIOSIS

I am staring at Rob Lowe, the actor. He smiles down at me, showing off a six pack. I tell the nurse that whoever thought of putting his poster on the ceiling above the treatment bed I am currently lying on deserves a medal! I stare intently into his piercing blue eyes. I am flirting with a poster, but trust me: if you saw the size of the needle you would also do anything to take your mind off the fact that this is shortly going to make its way into your belly. I'm here to get the first of my six monthly doses of GnRH injections. It's usually used to treat prostate cancer in men. As far as I understand, I will be injected with male hormones that will put my female reproductive system to sleep. Oh well, six months of no periods – got to be worth it.

The male hormones I now have instead of my female ones, have no idea about all the jobs the female hormones do. It's like my mum going on holiday and my dad not knowing how to switch on the dishwasher, where to put the washing powder in the machine or when to take the rubbish bins out. Things start getting a bit messy.

There are advantages and disadvantages to everything, GnRH injections are no exception. I LOVE my hot flushes. I am always cold, so being able to walk on the kitchen tiles bare footed with a glass of chilled white wine in my hand is the version of me I always wanted to be. Goodbye hot cup of tea and woolly night socks! Goodbye yeti woman! From now on just call me sex goddess. The only trouble is, my hot sexy body is just hot, not sexy. My libido has gone on holiday with the female hormones and is lounging about, blissfully enjoying a Piña Colada under a palm tree somewhere on the other side of the world.

My lush moist vaginal rain forest has turned into the Sahara desert. I go and buy some personal lubricant. While I enjoy not being in excruciating pain every month, I don't think I would want to live like this forever. My body feels like a piece of dead meat, all sensations have disappeared. Six months of my very own drought down below will be enough, and I am already looking forward to the monsoon season starting again.

My hormonal role reversal does give me time to reflect. I realize how utterly desperate my situation has become. When I was in constant pain, there was no space for reflection, awareness or self-realisation. I was in survival mode. The break from my monthly period allows me to look at myself and my situation with new eyes - the eyes of a peaceful observer, rather than the knight on the battlefield, fighting a war.

Millions of women like me exist all around the globe. We call ourselves *endo warriors*, fighting a monthly battle. Endometriosis pain is not unlike birthing contractions. Those primal screams you hear down the hospital corridors, when it is too late to give an epidural to a woman in labour, that's comparable to us. The only difference is, there is no cute baby to hold afterwards, no rush of oxytocin - the love hormone that lets you forget the ordeal. No minimum nine months pause between babies. Endo warriors get the pleasure of labour pain every month.

Every single month, someone is squeezing my inner organs until I nearly black out. For those seven to ten days my period tends to last, there is a dull base pain that constantly lurks in the background. That base pain almost feels like a safe harbour compared to the ferocious waves that wash over me and knock me off my feet mercilessly, especially the first couple of days of my period. 'Why can't I be a man?' In between the waves of pain that literally take my breath away, I plead with God, 'Please, just let me die. I can't stand this any longer!' I have always loved life, but each month when my period starts, I look at myself thinking, 'Who is this miserable, wretched wreck of a human? How did I turn into this?'

I constantly feel like a wimp and believe I have a lower pain threshold than others. My doctors tell me to take standard painkillers like Paracetamol or Ibuprofen, and to accept the pain as normal period pain. I try. I try so hard, but I KNOW that none of my friends seem to experience their periods as badly as this. I also constantly doubt my own judgement. Countless times, I allow the doctors to fob me off, to send me back into my silent, isolated suffering. Every month, I'm left exhausted, tired of fighting and of soldiering on.

Now that I finally have a proper diagnosis, I find out that I actually have a high pain threshold. – a consequence of being exposed to this level of pain every month. Our bodies apparently get used to pain. I remember going to a special acupressure therapist who asked me to tell him on a scale of one to ten how painful the pressure was that he was applying to my muscles, with one being hardly any pressure and ten being the most one could bear. The idea was, he would press until he got to ten, keep up the pressure, and then my constantly tense muscles would eventually relax by themselves, easing my pain. He kept pressing and I'd go, 'Mmh, I'd give that a two… now maybe a four' It took him ages to get to eight and he didn't have the strength to get to my ten. The bizarre thing is, I almost felt proud of this. 'See how much pain I can stand! I'm a true warrior!'

One in ten women is estimated to suffer from endometriosis. How had I never heard of it before now? In 2011, when I finally do get diagnosed, the majority of women (and doctors) in this world seem to have no idea this illness exists.

My recent diagnosis has put me on a discovery trail and I take my friends with me. My friend Anna is sitting opposite me at our local coffee shop. Each of us is cradling a large cafe latte. People are walking by outside the big glass windows, it's a rainy British day in spring. Now that I finally have a diagnosis, an actual illness that has its own name, I feel I can share my ordeal with my friends. The name gives my suffering validation.

> "Endo… what?" my friend says completely baffled, when I tell her what I've got. This is most people's reaction.

> "Endometriosis. Quite a mouthful, hey?" I laugh, trying to make light of my new label, "Apparently one in ten women suffer from it. You can call it endo for short. Even I can't remember its full name half the time."

"One in ten women have it? No way! How can this be? If that was true, we would have heard about it. We ARE women, after all."

"Well, would we though? Have heard about it, I mean? How often do you and I discuss our periods? I mean, I might have said 'I feel rubbish', but that would be it. And how am I to know that my period pain might be any more than yours. I mean, you always hear about PMT[2] and stuff, you just think every woman goes through the same and it's just what happens once a month."

"Well, I can honestly tell you that I've never felt like what you've just described! Christ!" Anna takes a sip of her latte. "Unbelievable! So you are saying, it takes an average of eight to ten years to get diagnosed? Gosh. If I think how many times you've been to a doctor. For years, they just told you to take paracetamol. You poor thing! All this time, you felt like a hypochondriac. All this time, you were made to believe you were just imagining things. Like you were wasting our healthcare system's valuable time. I'm so sorry! I had no idea… I feel like I should have been a better friend."

"Well, I never said anything because I guess I got told that lots of women experience period pains. And nobody can measure my pain against yours. There is no wimp to warrior pain scale. The

---

[2] PMT: pre-menstrual tension refers to slight discomfort, pain and tension in the lower abdomen before a period starts.

doctors always made me feel like my pain was normal and I was overreacting."

We both silently stare at our coffees. I think about all the times we haven't shared as friends, all those moments when I lacked the words to express what was going on inside me. I'm the first one to pull out of our mutual contemplation:

"So, I'm not a wimp, after all! You cannot imagine the relief I felt when I finally got a diagnosis. I'm not imagining things! I've got an actual illness that has a name. Even if we can't pronounce it!"

"What can they do?"

"Well, the doctor said the only thing is a hysterectomy. But I've done some research online and it looks like even that doesn't mean I'll be cured. In lots of cases endo seems to return after a few years, sometimes even months. If they catch it early, they can laser it away. Although even after lasering, it often comes back. In any case, my endo has spread too far for that. It's basically everywhere, covering my ovaries, my bowel, the outside of my womb. The consultant told me everything in there is just too red and angry to do anything right now. Her plan is to shut the system down for six months; and then she suggests a hysterectomy, where they take out the whole womb. So at the moment, I'm on these injections and they are great!... Well, actually they are not great, but they give me six months of no periods. I'll see after that. I'm not keen on the idea of a hysterectomy, but if it's got to be done, it's got to be done. Right now, I'll enjoy six months without period pain. Yeah!" I do a little pretend dance of joy and my friend laughs, although the concern still shows in her face.

"It's what they call a chronic illness. I'm just going to have to live with it." Our eyes connect. We are back where we should be as friends.

"For most women it gets better once you hit menopause. I'm only 34… but maybe I reach menopause early, like 42 or something. That would mean I'd have to just survive another eight years." I cringe at the thought of another eight years of this.

CHAPTER 4
DIFFERENT COUNTRIES, DIFFERENT WAYS

I am crouching on the bathroom floor again. The guy who put it in was really pleased when he found some reclaimed timber we could recycle. It looks lovely and warm when the sun shines in through the window in the morning. Right now, however, it is a freezing cold wooden floor. It is 2.30am in winter. I'm rolled together like a ball, holding my tummy, trying to breathe and relax my muscles that have gone into spasm. Something is different to my normal period pain. I feel like one of my cysts might have burst. Ovarian cysts, or endometriomas, are another very common symptom of endometriosis. I have two cysts and they vary in size but are usually around 4.5-5cm in diameter. They are a bit like mini balloons filled with dark, old blood that looks like melted chocolate, which is why they are often called chocolate cysts. The pain I'm in right now is even more unbearable than normal, if that's at all possible. I'm nauseous and scared.

It's Sunday. Of course it's Sunday. You never feel really bad during the week when you can get hold of your general practitioner or gynaecologist. These things always happen on a Sunday. To make things worse, I'm supposed to fly to Germany tomorrow. There is no way I can fly in the state I'm in right now. I can't even stand upright. I'm wondering whether to go to A&E, when I remember that my gynaecologist actually gave me her email address at our last meeting. Could I send her an email on a Sunday? I don't think I can. There must be an unwritten rule about respecting a doctor's weekend privacy? Besides, what is she going to do on a Sunday anyway? After an internal dialogue that goes on for hours, I decide to send an email.

> Dear Mrs Myers,
>
> Sorry to disturb you on a Sunday, but I just don't know what to do. I'm in really bad pain. Is it possible one of my cysts has burst? I'm supposed to go to Germany tomorrow morning and I might be able to see my gynaecologist there. Is it safe to fly if a cyst has burst?
> Could you see me tomorrow and do an ultrasound to find out what's going on? This is much worse than anything I've had before.
> I do apologise for disturbing your Sunday!
>
> Kind regards,
> Emmie

I get a reply within the hour.

> Dear Emmie
>
> It's half term next week and my ultrasound specialist is on holiday, so I would not be able to get a clear picture of what's going on until the week after. It's unlikely to be a burst cyst and even if it is, you should be ok to fly. If you want to book in for the week after next, please ring the hospital reception to make an appointment.
> I suggest you fly to Germany and try to get an ultrasound there, if you can. By the sound of it, this would be much quicker.
>
> Best Wishes,
> Mrs Myers

I've lived in England for years, but as my grandmother died of cervical cancer I go for a gynaecological check-up in Germany once a year, rather than relying on the three-year smear test offered by the British medical system. Gynaecologists in Germany tend to work in their own private practice, with the latest equipment and technology. It's sterile and clean, yet comfortable without the hospital anonymity. Thanks to a friend, I am able to get hold of my German gynaecologist even though it's Sunday. As a favour to our mutual friend, she agrees to squeeze me into her schedule the next day.

I dose up on painkillers and board the plane. My pain has decreased enough to make the flight just about bearable, I'm still incredibly worried and tense. My awareness is focused inwards and everything outside of my body ceases to exist. It's me, my pain and the single thought of wanting to just get to my appointment in Germany. Inhale. Exhale. Repeat.

The journey is a blur and I only snap out of my inner breathing meditation when I finally arrive at the practice. There are flower pots on the window sill, colourful blinds and the centre of the examination room is a proper gynaecological chair in a warm, green leather. It's one of those where you sit back comfortably while your legs are akimbo and elevated, putting your pelvis in the perfect position and tilt for a vaginal examination. My bottom is resting on the towel I brought with me. The practice is equipped with two ultrasound machines, one for internal vaginal examination and one for the abdomen and breasts. Large, clear screens positioned for easy viewing show me big images of the scan in real time. My doctor talks to me whilst examining me, explaining exactly what she sees.

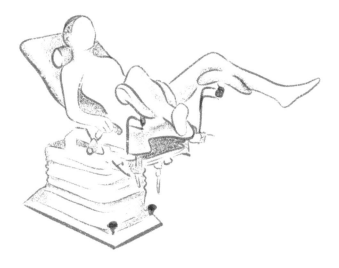

For the same examination in England, I would need three separate appointments: one with my gynaecologist, a second with the sonographer and a third with the gynaecologist again to get the results. I remember once asking the sonographer what she saw while she was examining me, and she would not give me the slightest indication. I'd had a flare up and was incredibly worried until my result's appointment with the gynaecologist finally came along a couple of weeks later. In Germany, it's all done in one appointment at a third of the price I paid privately in Britain.

I haven't seen Dr. Westermann since my official diagnosis of endometriosis. She is incredibly supportive, listening to my proposed plan of action: GnRH injections and then a possible hysterectomy. As luck would have it, she wrote her doctorate on endometriosis. That alone makes me feel in good hands, and I relax into a feeling of relief and trust. After the examination, we sit in her office, separated by a wooden desk with family pictures on it. She looks me straight in the eye and calmly says,

> "You know, you can manage endometriosis with nutrition."

There is a pause while she waits for my reaction. I'm not sure what I'm feeling. Disbelief? Shock? Hope? I'm motionless, so she carries on:

> "If you want my advice, have the injections for six months. It will give you time to make changes in your life. Under no circumstances have them longer than six months. They massively impact your body, especially your bone density further down the line. There are studies that show severe osteoporosis in women 20 years post hysterectomy. Unfortunately, it's not the easy solution it may appear to be."

I listen in utter astonishment as she continues. All this is new to me.

> "The GnRH injections can buy you time. Use that time to do some research, and look into nutrition. My advice would be to not have a hysterectomy, if you can avoid it. It should really be your very last resort. If they take the ovaries out, you'd be put on HRT (Hormone Replacement Therapy) and at 34 you're really too young for that. If the ovaries are left in, they would carry on releasing hormones and you would most likely experience endometriosis pain even after the surgery, as the pockets of endometriosis cells outside the womb will still be there, reacting to the hormones exactly as they do now. In addition, you might open yourself up to a whole array of hysterectomy side effects that could be almost as unpleasant as your endometriosis. So you may just be swapping one lot of problems for another."

I leave gob smacked. Nutrition? How could something as simple as nutrition sort out my pain? I was told I needed a hysterectomy and that there may be a very unlikely but possible need to remove part of my bowel, and here I am told I can simply avoid certain foods? While half of me does an optimistic somersault at the prospect of such a manageable solution, the other half looks on with great scepticism. Surely if this was a way out, my British doctor would have known about it? If endometriosis is an illness that affects one in ten women and a gynaecologist specializes in women's health, they would know, wouldn't they? The sceptical part of me is too exhausted and scared to hope, the optimist in me is clinging onto a tiny light that suddenly appears at the end of this very dark tunnel.

I start googling the minute I get back to my mum's house and come across a book by Dr. Dian Shepperson-Mills called 'Endometriosis: A key to healing through nutrition.'[3] That's encouraging. Clearly my German gynaecologist is not the only one aware of a nutritional approach to endometriosis. Perhaps there truly is something to it. I order the book and it's waiting for me as I get back to England.

Each month I go back to see Rob Lowe's poster and get my GnRH injections. I'm am eternally grateful for the breathing space they give me to study my illness. Dian Shepperson Mill's book becomes my endo bible. If you suffer from endometriosis, are a bookworm like me, and if you like getting to the bottom of things and want to understand what exactly is going on in your endo stricken body, I highly recommend reading it. It is incredibly detailed and explains the science in an understandable way.

I become my own guinea pig. I cut out gluten, sugar and dairy. After six months of GnRH injections, I feel good enough to

---

[3] Dian Shepperson Mills & Michael Vernon: Endometriosis. A Key to Healing and Fertility Through Nutrition. Thorsons, 2002. (There is a new edition now available from 2023).

postpone the hysterectomy indefinitely. My English gynaecologist agrees to monitor me at regular intervals. A few months after the injections stop, endo comes back with a vengeance. My body is once again wrecked with pain while my endo dragon rears its head every month and shouts 'How dare you try to get rid of me. I'll show you who is boss!'

The difference is, I have a newfound hope. I have got enough knowledge now to carry on with my experiment. I know my enemy. That hope generates an incredible will within me to live and fight. I am going to put on my knight's armour and I will win this war. Of that I am absolutely certain. I find local alternative practitioners and I build my own endometriosis war cabinet around me. My homeopath looks at my immune system and gives me mental and emotional support. My Chinese practitioner does acupuncture and prescribes the most foul smelling tea concoctions. My iridologist looks into my eyes and gives me my personal blueprint of health and as she also happens to be a nutritionist, she helps me sort out my dietary changes. My Bowen therapist helps release the tension I carry in every muscle due to the pain.

I spend an absolute fortune on appointments, opinions, treatments and supplements, but what price can you put on your health? I become obsessed with wanting to keep my body intact. My organs are mine! Slowly, I am regaining control over my life and managing my endometriosis. The first two days of my period are still extremely painful, but with the highest dose of paracetamol and ibuprofen taken in 3-4 hour intervals, using a vitamin B complex, Serrapeptase enzymes that help eliminate scar tissue, magnesium spray, and various other supplements, I manage.

List of Alternative Approaches to Healing

Homeopathy: Homeopathy is a type of complementary or alternative medicine that's based on the use of highly diluted substances, which practitioners claim can cause the body to heal itself.
(https://www.nhs.uk/conditions/homeopathy/)

TCM (Traditional Chinese Medicine): TCM is a system of medicine that aims to prevent or heal disease by maintaining or restoring yin-yang-balance. It is one of the oldest medical systems, which includes acupuncture and Chinese herbal remedies that date back over 2200 years.
(htpp://www.britannica.com/science/traditional-chinese-medicine)

Iridology: Iridology is an alternative medicine technique which claims that patterns, colours, and other characteristics of the eye's iris can be examined to determine information about a patient's systemic health. Practitioners use iris charts, which divide the iris into zones that correspond to specific parts of the body. The eyes are seen as "windows" into the body's state of health.
(https://en.wikipedia.org/wiki/Iridology)

Bowen Therapy: Bowen Therapy is an alternative type of physical manipulation. It involves gentle rolling motions across the muscles, tendons and fascia. Distinctive pauses help the body to reset itself.

> **Most Important Supplements for Endometriosis That Helped Me:**
>
> Vitamin B Complex
> Serrapeptase
> Magnesium (best as spray)
> Epsom Salt (as a bath additive)

I'm lucky that my periods are as regular as clock work. I tend to start bleeding on a Thursday evening, so I make sure I don't work on Fridays. At this stage, being able to be a mom to my son, a wife to my husband and earning a bit of money teaching business German part-time is all I aspire to. I resign myself to a life as an endometriosis sufferer. I believe that endo will be a part of me until menopause stops the release of oestrogen, putting an end to my monthly periods and my pain. It's not the full on happy, fulfilled life I had imagined myself living, but at least I feel a bit more balanced. Instead of endometriosis controlling my every move, we have reached a ceasefire.

My British gynaecologist agrees to monitor me, but she is worried and tells me so every time I see her. She fears that my endometriosis is secretly spreading inside and she still feels a hysterectomy is the safest way forward. Whilst I can understand her point of view and her concerns, I am just not ready to go down that route.

Why do I refuse to have a hysterectomy? My husband and many of my friends ask me this constantly. Why am I so stubborn? Why don't I just do what the doctor says? Why would I not at least go back on the contraceptive pill, which would most likely give some relief? Like my English gynaecologist, my family and friends are losing patience with me. For several days every month they helplessly witness my suffering: curled up on the sofa with a hot water bottle, on the highest dose of paracetamol and ibuprofen. They love me, and it hurts to see someone you love suffer, especially when there is nothing they can do to help me. I accept, that they don't understand my rejection of all the mainstream solutions. I just can't go against my own feelings, even if staying true to them means alienating everyone around me.

I am morphing into a 'lone endo warrior' on a healing mission. It would be so much easier to just turn around and float in the current of conformism. My former lack of awareness and lack of medical knowledge is turning into a deeper understanding for my own body, as I'm reading and studying my illness. The alternative approaches have opened a door into a new world I can't ignore, now that I know it exists. I also have my own and my family's experiences that form part of my decision to not listen to my doctors. There are effectively four reasons why I refuse to have a hysterectomy.

Reason No. 1: My mother had a hysterectomy at the age of forty two, after years of suffering from very similar symptoms (although there wasn't a diagnosable illness called endometriosis in those days). She subsequently struggled all her life to balance her hormone levels, often feeling drained and exhausted as a result. She developed osteoporosis, a common side effect of hysterectomies. In her sixties, she got diagnosed with thyroid cancer. There is an increased risk of thyroid cancer in women who have undergone hysterectomies. Unlike so many other women who blindly agree to hysterectomies as the proposed solution to endometriosis, I know thanks to my mum, that it isn't the easy way out. There are life-changing implications that I would most likely face as a direct result of an irreversible hysterectomy.

I read on online endometriosis forums that many women who chose to have hysterectomies, end up with the same pain again after two to three years, finding themselves back at square one, just without their womb. Other women report bladder issues as a result of the hysterectomy, one problem simply replacing another. Our organs are tightly nestled together in a perfect puzzle; removing a womb leaves a gap that surrounding organs can collapse into.

Yes, for some women, having a hysterectomy really helps and solves their problem. However, the statistics are just not good enough to persuade me.

Reason No. 2: My father was diagnosed with stage IV colon cancer at the age of fifty four and was left with a colostomy bag. Even the remotest possibility of anyone touching my bowel makes me want to run. I know that stomas have an automatic air release mechanism that means farting noises at any point in your day, regardless of whether you are in a public restaurant having a meal with friends, or in a meeting with a client. I know that stomas sometimes come undone accidentally, leaving you covered in your own excrement while out getting your supermarket shopping. I know what massive psychological trauma having to live with a stoma caused my dad. I know that most likely my operation would never result in me having to live like my dad, but there is no way I am going to take the risk. You just never know. However good a surgeon might be, things can always go wrong. No, thank you, I'd rather have a few days of pain every month. Better the devil you know.

Reason No. 3: My grandmother died of cervical cancer. During pregnancy with my son, I experienced some bleeding around week twenty, mid-way through. I was admitted to hospital but the baby seemed well and it was decided to leave further investigations until I had given birth. When I finally went for a check-up, several months later, pre-cancerous cells were discovered on my cervix. These were duly removed and I was given the 'all clear'. Looking into the side effects of the contraceptive pill I had used to manage my period pains for twelve years before getting pregnant, an increased risk of cervical cancer was on the list. Going back to taking the pill isn't an option anymore.

Reason No. 4: This is the one I find hardest to articulate, even though it is probably the most important motivator for my stubbornness. As a thinking, reasoning human being, having grown up in an era that admires the scientific advances we have made in medicine, I feel I can't tell anyone what my gut feeling is telling me I can heal naturally. There is a voice in my head that whispers very clearly: 'Do not have the operation!' Deep down, it just doesn't feel right. Everything inside me recoils at the thought of having a part of my body taken. Deep down, I am convinced I can win my endo war without surgical intervention.

I know in my heart that there is another way out of this and just because I can't see it yet, doesn't mean it's not there. My intuition gives me the courage and strength to keep swimming against the tide. This inner belief is so strong, I cannot ignore it, however much I sometimes wish I could. For now, my endometriosis doesn't seem to be getting any worse. That's all that counts. There is hope. I will find a way, I just have to keep searching.

CHAPTER 5
BEING SILENCED - LOSING MY VOICE

Is my endometriosis truly not getting worse? Am I just lying to myself out of fear for what the alternative would be? What would happen if I admitted to myself and the world that actually, deep down, I am not alright? I am too wrapped up in my endo war to mentally go there. I am managing a fragile ceasefire, and I know the full blown war in my tummy can explode in all its might the minute I take my eye of the ball. I am an endo warrior. I mustn't show weakness. I mustn't show fear. Or my enemy will get me.

I become a master of deception. To the outside world, my life is fine. I hide the truth from everyone, even myself. All I have to do is somehow get through my fertile, productive years of being a woman. Menopause will come. I cannot wait to greet it. I will welcome it with open arms. Menopause. The prince in shining armour, who will eventually come to slay my fire spewing endo dragon. I carry on fighting every month to not let endo take over my life. Although, if I am honest with myself, endo is fully in charge. Everything I do is planned and scheduled meticulously around my cycle. I know when I ovulate, I know when my period is about to start, I know when the pain will be dull but bearable and when to keep my diary free of appointments as I'll be confined to my bed or sofa, cradling a hot water bottle, drugged up on pain killers. I know the days each month, when I am unavailable to life. I know how many days it takes my body to calm down the inflammation. I know what time each month I will re-emerge from my torture chamber, pretending all is well in my world.

Holidays, cinema visits, meeting friends… as long as I plan things carefully, nobody knows what pain I'm in every month. The happy, healthy human being most people get to see is but a hologram. The true me is hiding somewhere deep inside, so well camouflaged even I cannot spot her anymore. As time goes by, I forget who I was before I became an endo warrior. Just like the world around me, I am starting to believe the hologram is me.

My deception strategy works until October 2013. I have a bad chest infection. I cough night and day and after a week or so, I lose my voice. I don't think much of it. It's quite a common symptom when you go down with a bad autumn cold. After about three weeks, my body has fully recovered, except for my voice. When my voice is still hoarse three months later, it occurs to me that I should probably consult a doctor to see what is going on. A camera up my nostril and down my throat shows a tiny little growth on my left vocal cord. The Ear, Nose & Throat (ENT) consultant seems unconcerned.

> "It's a tiny little polyp. A very common thing for singers and teachers, any people who work with their voice, really," he explains. "I can schedule you in for a little operation called a laryngoscopy. We go in through your mouth and throat into your voice box and surgically remove the polyp. It's not a big thing. You come in in the morning, you go home in the afternoon. Two weeks voice rest, maybe a bit of speech therapy afterwards. You will be back to normal in no time."

I look at him. Smile. Given my endometriosis battle, I haven't got the nerve or strength to research or question this second health issue that has popped up from seemingly nowhere. I cannot fight two wars. I agree to have the operation. At this point in my story, I don't know yet that developing a second chronic illness is very common for women suffering from endometriosis. The immune system is so weakened by the monthly inflammation, it simply cannot deal with anything else. This often opens the door for other chronic illnesses, often autoimmune diseases.

My first laryngoscopy arrives. It's a quick in and out day job. My surgeon removes the little growth. I recover. My life resumes. Briefly. A check-up six months later finds more growths on my vocal cords. My consultant seems unperturbed:

> "Sometimes this happens. It's very rare and in the vast majority of patients a second operation clears the problem once and for all. I'll book you in for another day case. We will do exactly what we did before and surgically remove the growth."

Too exhausted to argue, I agree to my second laryngoscopy. In and out in a day. Voice rest. Speech therapy. My private speech therapist charges eighty pounds for half an hour and teaches me to breathe. What a total rip off! Surely we all know how to breathe! The 2013 version of me doesn't yet understand that breathing connects me to my life force. I am unaware of the power of pranayama, the practice of breath regulation and its magical effect on the human body. Instead of feeling grateful for having been introduced to the magic of correct breathing, the 2013 version of me is fuming at the total waste of my money and time. I am so tired, so very tired of being ill. In my ignorance (or desperate exhaustion), I am trusting the conventional medical system. I long to lead a normal life. I long for a life far away from hospital appointments, consultant rooms and kind, smiling nurses.

Another six monthly check-up reveals a new sprouting of growths. Little mushroom like shapes sitting neatly on my vocal cords, hindering the vibrational movement that produces what we call speech. It's not a disaster, I am speaking, but my voice sounds hoarse and it's hurting to speak sometimes. Operation two reveals that the polyps are not polyps, but papillomas, a much more difficult growth to get rid of, not dissimilar to a wart. Great! Warts on my vocal cords are just what I needed.

Papillomas are caused by the Human Papilloma Virus (HPV). HPV is a virus 95% of humans get infected with at some stage during their adult, sexually active life. It's a virus that can lie dormant for decades, waiting for the immune system to weaken before it rears its nasty head. Areas it can affect are varied, one of those areas happens to be the throat. When it affects the vocal cords, the diagnosis goes on the medical record as laryngeal papillomatosis. Another mouthful, not much easier to pronounce or remember than endometriosis.

When I was pregnant with my son, I had an episode of bleeding at about 20 weeks, caused by changed cells on my cervix. The cells were removed after I had given birth. I remember someone mentioning HPV as a cause for cervical cell changes. Could the growths on my vocal cords be linked to the changed cells on my cervix? Can they move through the body? Can I somehow have done something to move them from the cervix to the throat? Oral sex? Is there anything I should or shouldn't be doing? When I dare to ask these question, the consultant actually blushes, while stuttering that his area of expertise is the throat, not the cervix. Clearly for him, I am not a human being consisting of connected body parts, but an isolated growth on the vocal cord.

Within the medical system, I am now classified as a chronic case. Stick on the label, into the drawer I go. My private consultant can no longer look after me, my private health insurance no longer likes me. Chronic conditions need regular intervention which cost money, they are a bottomless pit. Papillomas seem almost impossible to treat. People with my condition require regular operations, some have them every six to eight weeks. I get referred to a specialist Ear, Nose & Throat unit at my local National Health Service (NHS) hospital. I am now a chronic voice condition: a new hospital, a new consultant, a new set of kind, smiling nurses.

There is another caveat. Officially now the proud owner of a second chronic illness, I get to add a new vicious cycle to my repertoire. After each full anaesthetic, my endometriosis flares up with a vengeance. My womb and vocal cords are bouncing on a seesaw of pain, as one is up, the other is down. By the time each endo flare-up is back under control, the next voice operation is on the cards. One chronic illness hands the baton over to the other in a perpetual relay race of who can make my life more miserable. The optimist in me is slowly morphing into a parody version of herself, desperate to still laugh at the burlesque my life is becoming, desperate to believe in the full recovery the doctors keep promising me so wholeheartedly. Fool's gold.

I like my new consultant. I trust his judgement. He advises operation number three. More voice rest, more speech therapy and I am almost back to normal. What a success! Extremely pleased with the outcome of operation three, my surgeon enthusiastically suggests operation four: "I removed all the growths on your left vocal cord. But there are still some little ones on the right cord. When the vocal cords heal, some scarring or webbing occurs. We don't operate on both cords at the same time, as there is a risk of webbing forming between the cords, and they obviously need to vibrate freely. I suggest we do one very last operation on the right vocal cord. Given the success we've had, I'm confident this will be the end of it." My voice is so much better after operation three. Clearly this consultant knows what he is doing. Having one last laryngoscopy will restore both cords and allow me to live my life happily ever after. It's the stuff fairy tales are made of.

How I wish I had just left it at operation three. But as humans we are greedy, aren't we? Operation four turns the promise of my fairy-tale ending into an absolute nightmare. Two operations in six months are too much for my endometriosis riddled, weakened body and my whole voice apparatus shuts down. I am in constant endometriosis induced agony and no speech therapy or breathing can get my cords to vibrate in any way that would produce sound.

For the first two weeks of silence, my friends still pop round and phone, happy to entertain me with their monologues. Three weeks in, the phone no longer rings. It's as silent as the front door bell and my larynx. My husband is rubbish at reading my sign language and retreats into his men's world, while my son amazes me with his wizard like ability to understand perfectly what desire my gulping fish mouth is trying to express. He seems to have the ability to magically tune into my thoughts and read my mind. I have always had a telepathic connection with my dad. As one would think of the other, the phone would miraculously ring. 'I was just thinking of you!', or 'How did you know I was just about to phone you?' The way Jack understands me without words takes this telepathic parent-child connection to another level. It's spooky how he knows exactly what I need without any words needing to travel from my voice box through the ether to his ears. Whatever vibrational signals are being sent to enable a message exchange between us, they are not of the kind usually used in this world. My son becomes the only one I communicate with, the rest of the world retreats.

Or is it me who retreats from the world? Going outside means people wanting to speak and communicate. I feel self-conscious and awkward not being able to say anything. I smile. I make funny gestures indicating I have no voice. I choose deserted fields over the park for my dog walks and I learn to avoid humans. After six eternal weeks without any voice whatsoever, I finally manage to get an emergency appointment with my consultant. I sit in front of him with the little notebook that has become my life line to the outside world.

He looks at me quizzically: "Mmh, medically the operation has been a success. All the growths have been removed. I think the fact you can't speak must by psychosomatic." I sit there staring at him in disbelief. I am so shell shocked at his words, I can't even cry. In my little mermaid silence, I scribble on my notebook page: "How can it be a success, if I cannot speak at all?" He looks at me with pity and repeats like a parrot: "Medically the operation has been a success. There are no growths on your vocal cords."

It's beyond my comprehension, how anyone can call something a success that so clearly is a massive, fat failure. Surely the whole point of these operations was to restore my voice, not to produce clean, tidy vocal cords that are defunct. It's another glimpse at the absurdity of our current medical system, which does not measure success according to a patient's quality of life, but according to some artificial parameters only science seems to understand. Parameters that often seem as far removed from life as one can get.

So here I am, a silent medical success. A little mermaid, who sold her voice for the promise of a prince that never notices her for who she truly is. If you are familiar with Anderson's fairy tale *The Little Mermaid*, you will know that she sells her voice to a witch, who transforms her fish tail into human feet. But every step she takes on her human feet feels like she is walking on nails. My throat feels like I've swallowed a cup of nails. After six weeks of total silence, I am able to whisper a few words, each one a gigantic effort accompanied by razor sharp pains cutting the inside of my throat.

CHAPTER 6
DARK NIGHT OF THE SOUL

I'm trapped in my own body. Trapped in what is starting to become a very dark place deep inside myself. Have you ever heard the phrase 'the only way out is in'? It pops up when people describe spiritual journeys. I don't know it yet, but this is the start of my own deeply spiritual journey. 'In' is literally the only way I can go. Going 'in' is not a choice, however, it becomes utter torture. My optimist turns pessimist and the world around me drowns in darkness. Inside myself, I am trapped in the dungeon of my own fears. What if I'll never speak again?

My inner optimist chimes in, the tiniest speck of light, a spark in the blackness of my own hopelessness: I'll just have to learn sign language. Will my husband and son have to learn sign language? Would I get a job translating theatre performances into sign language? Can you do justice to Shakespeare's genius with words in sign language? I research sign language courses near me, so I'm prepared for the future.

"Don't be silly," my optimist chides. "Your voice will come back, you'll be fine. Trust." The little spark of optimism is struggling to bring light into my existence. I spiral deeper and deeper into the black hole of my own despair, buried alive inside the inner workings of my own mind. Every day, after dropping my son off at the school gate and walking the dog, I return home, collapse on the brown leather sofa in our lounge and cry uncontrollable, silent sobs, our springadore Buster the only witness to my desolation.

Every single day, I cry until my eyes run dry and my body has no strength to shake anymore. My inner saboteurs hatch a plan.

Their voice becomes stronger and louder inside my head: "We can end this. It will be fine. Nobody wants a silent endo warrior in their lives. Everyone would be much better off without you." Their advice sounds reasonable. In fact, it sounds like bliss. No more pain. No more life. The next six months, I spend planning. It feels great to have a purpose again, even if the purpose is how to best stop being a human on this planet.

Pills. I look through the cupboards and find Paracetamol, Ibuprofen and Co-codamol. Would they be strong enough to kill me? How many would I need? At the supermarket I am not allowed to buy more than two packs at a time. I will definitely need more than two. I've put away nine packs at the moment. I will get more. Would painkillers work as a life terminator, or would I need sleeping pills? The universe always gives you what you want: a couple of weeks later, an elderly friend hands me a plastic bag with out of date medication and asks me to kindly return them to the pharmacy for her. I keep the bag. I hide it in the top left cupboard in the spare bedroom, with the nine packs of painkillers. There is even a bottle of morphine in the bag, unused. Surely, altogether, that should be enough.

What will it be like to die from an overdose of pills? It must feel horrible, I taste their bitterness in my imagination. Will the stomach contract in pain? Will there be seizures before it's all over? I've got to make sure I don't vomit and I must do it when I know nobody would find me prematurely. The last thing I want is to be rushed into hospital. The last thing I want is for the plan to fail.

Train. The news this morning reported someone threw themselves in front of a tube in London again. I'm at my local village train station waiting for the train into town. The voice coming out of the loudspeaker asks passengers to step back from the track. On platform one an express train is passing through the station. I'm almost blown off my feet by the winds created as the train torpedoes passed me. Maybe that might work? If I step off the platform and time it right, there is nothing anyone could do. Death would be certain, and quick. I think about the train driver. I've heard about the psychological impact it has on them, when their train kills another human. It may ruin their life. I start writing a letter to the train driver that will potentially kill me:

> Dear train driver,
>
> I'm sorry! Please do not feel guilty about killing me. It was my own wish to end my life and jumping in front of your train seemed the quickest, surest way of actually succeeding. When you read this, I will be dead. Please promise me that you will enjoy life. Live life for both of us. And promise me you won't feel guilty. This has nothing to do with you.

Should I end with 'Love' or with 'Kind regards'? What's the appropriate form of address in a suicide note? I better also write a note for my husband and my son. Oh, how I will miss them! I can feel the pain of their loss in my heart imagining them without me. I'm thinking about the phone ringing, someone on the other hand giving my husband the news. Him having to tell our son. Again. A déjà vu of love lost. Again, a dad telling his son that his mum had died and would never ever wake him up in the morning, smile at him, laugh with him, or just make him a slice of buttered toast. My husband lost his first wife to cancer, so he has done this once before.

It breaks my heart thinking about putting my husband through this again. But then my inner saboteurs tells me, he will get over it. Just like he got over the death of his first wife, he'll get over my death. Just like he met me, he'll meet wife number three. And she'll be healthy and happy, not the pain ridden, voiceless shadow of a human I currently am. Just like his two older sons carried on living after their mum had passed away, our son will carry on living after I'm gone. Everyone will be better off without me. Weeks and weeks pass this way. Thinking up suicide scenarios becomes the most natural pastime. How to end life becomes the sole purpose of my sad, wretched existence. There is no beauty left to see. I no longer hear the birdsong. I no longer see the butterflies. I no longer feel the warmth of the sun in the sky.

Day after day, week after week, month after month, I am trapped at the bottom of a deep, dark well. The well is only in my mind, but it's so real I can smell and taste it. Everything around me disappears into pitch dark blackness, I can't see the walls of the well, but I know they are there. A round circle of stones, large enough so I can sit with my legs outstretched at the very bottom of the well. I know it's a well, because when I look up - a long way up - I can see a tiny spot of light. It's unreachably far from where I am. I know that up there, where that tiny spot of light is, life happens. I know that up there people are going about their day to day business of being human. I silently scream.

"HELLO! I'm down here! HELLO!"

If only I could get someone's attention, they could throw a rope down and get me out of here. Only silence echoes back at me. I've got no voice. Everybody is busy living their own lives. Nobody looks down into the well. Even if they did, they would not notice me. I'm so deep down, no spark of light could penetrate the dark night engulfing my soul. A thought forms. It's a tiny whisper of a thought.

> "Start climbing."
> "Climbing? There is no way I'd have the strength to climb up there!"
> "Well, nobody else will save you. You either do it yourself or…"

"I can't! Look at it! It's too far up. Even if I get half way up, what if I fall?"

I curl my legs up and cradle them, lying on the naked stone floor, my chest pressed into my thighs. I am the night. I am the darkness. I am the silence.

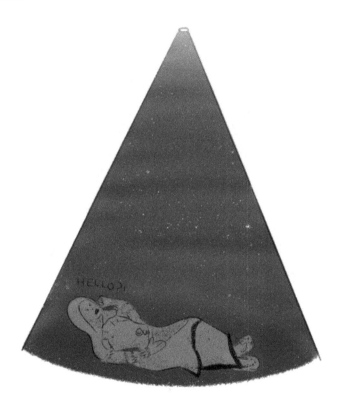

PART TWO
HEALING

"Ask and it will be given to you; seek and you will find; knock and the door will be opened to you." (Bible, Matthew 7:7-8)

CHAPTER 7
REIKI – MY FIRST STEP TO INNER PEACE

My existence has become a two week cycle. Two weeks of endometriosis pain, two weeks of no pain… two weeks of endometriosis pain, two weeks of no pain. I need to do something. I don't know what. But I need to somehow help myself.

Among those initiated into the teachings of Reiki, it is said that Reiki finds you, when the time is right. Reiki is a Japanese energy healing technique, where energy is channelled or sent through the hands of the practitioner into the recipient's energy field. You may have heard of people 'healing with their hands' or of 'laying on hands' – a practice that exists in various cultures all over the world: Reiki is pretty much that. In spring 2016, I receive an email from my local health food shop advertising a Reiki course twenty minutes away. It is advertised as a course for self-healing. Self-healing is exactly what I need.

It's not the first time I've heard the word Reiki. Two years previously, a massage therapist I saw regularly mentioned that she also did Reiki treatments. Curious to experience new things, I agreed to give it a go. I felt totally relaxed, although I knew the therapist had not touched my body at all. No contact had been made. It felt like I was floating. As I slowly came back into the room after nearly an hour of treatment, she asked me if I was pregnant, as she could feel a dense energy in my womb. I had never talked to her about suffering from endometriosis, so I was absolutely astounded that she had picked up on something going on in precisely the area where I was hurting. I was intrigued, but part of me found it a little spooky how she could pick up on my energies and I never went back for another Reiki treatment.

Yet, here I am, two years later, in a little village in the English countryside, sitting on a square Moroccan meditation cushion in a circle of women I have never met before. Just 30 minutes from where I live, I have entered another world. There is no rational explanation for the warmth in my heart that seems to say 'This is where you belong'.

Our Reiki teachers are talking to us about energy, how we can connect to energy, feel it, and use it to bring balance into our energy fields. It seems totally bizarre, that through mere intention and focus I should be able to guide the flow of any energy. I am utterly amazed by the energy I can feel running through my hands and through the room. There is tingling, heat, energy simmering in mid-air like it does on a hot summer's day. I can see it clearly, even though we are inside and the temperature is normal.

Practicing on ourselves and on each other, we learn about the energy field around us, the energy fields between us, and how Reiki practitioners believe that energy is the key to illness and healing. The belief is that any physical illness is preceded by an imbalance in the energy field. This imbalance can be re-balanced, recreating harmony in the body's energy system, before a physical illness can manifest. If you are already ill, re-balancing the energy system around you supports the body's healing process. I imagine the energy field is like a mould that the physical body forms in. If the energetic mould is not at ease (diseased), the physical body manifesting in that mould won't be at ease either. An operation might bring short term relief, but unless we change the energetic blueprint, the disease will come back or another illness will appear.

This is a whole new, mind-blowing world for me. A new way of looking at the body, at healing and at my own illnesses. My inner voice of reason tells me this is all rubbish. There is no way, I could ever talk to my husband or my friends about this: they would all think I was mad! My gut feeling tells a different story. Its little voice whispers from deep within myself.

> LITTLE VOICE: "This is real! ... This is the truth! ... This makes sense."
> [Little voice covers its mouth with its hands, shocked that it has spoken.]
> "Everything you are hearing and learning is true."
>
> VOICE OF REASON: "Rubbish! If anyone saw us, they'd laugh at us! Be quiet!"

Quiet! I silence my Voice of Reason. Something I haven't done in a long time. Right here, sitting on the Moroccan meditation cushion with all its earthy colours and geometric mandala shapes, I feel too at ease to listen to Voice of Reason. Just allow me this one day! One day of not feeling my aching body, please.

In a coffee break, I pick up a book from the shelf. It's all about energy meridians crisscrossing the human body. Humans have believed in energy systems for thousands of years. We are mind, body and spirit, and the spirit is the energy we are. The Indian chakra system, Chinese acupuncture - there has to be a reason this knowledge has been passed on from generation to generation. As a species, we are too intelligent to keep something alive that does not work, so there must be something to it, mustn't there?

To relax enough to connect to the energy, to find tranquillity and inner calm, we are meditating. I haven't felt this relaxed for years. It feels like my inside is expanding. I suddenly realise just how stressed I am in my everyday life, how tense my body is pretty much everywhere, all the time. As I am following the soothing music playing in the background, I feel total peace. All my limbs and even my jaw relax into the space around me.

We treat each other and in utter amazement I become aware how different people's energies feel. At no point am I actually touching the person I am working on, my hands hover about four inches above their body. How is it possible, I am feeling all these differences? There are eight of us in the class and when we talk about our treatments afterwards, we discover that we all experience the energy differently. Some of us see colours, some feel pressure and tingling, and others receive strong visions and pictures in their mind. Whatever the person treating feels, seems to tie in with the person that is being treated. There seems to be an undeniable connection. Could it all be illusion? It feels so real, so true, so right.

In the meditative Reiki space, I feel connected with my true self. I don't have to justify my experience to anyone. I am free to just be. No rationalising. No thinking. No worrying. No explaining. While my Voice of Reason shouts 'Rubbish! You're just making it up,' my heart sings 'I am home!'

I finish my Level One Reiki course, eager to further explore the new world of energy I have discovered. A month of daily practice and two in-person training days have changed my world forever. How does it work? How can I feel what I'm feeling? How is it possible to perceive all these energy differences between people? I delve into quantum physics, as this seems the best place to study energies. My rational brain wants to understand the science behind my totally irrational experiences. I begin reading Carlo Rovelli's relatively easy books on quantum physics, before turning to Einstein and Stephen Hawking.[4] I am amazed by how spiritual these scientists are in the way they see the world.

I am confronted with my own judgments, my own prejudices, my own antiquated belief systems, my own limitations. On the one hand, my voice of reason wants to doubt and discredit all the things I am experiencing. On the other hand, I have a seemingly insatiable hunger for more, and my pioneer spirit is dying to explore this unknown world further. My soul is longing to remember itself. Every day gets born every morning, and dies every night in a twilight zone. Light and dark eternally turning into each other. Reiki is opening the door to a new awareness, a new possibility, a turning point.

There are five precepts in Reiki. Similar to the Ten Commandments in the bible, these precepts give me guidance. They become part of my daily routine and I recite them before doing my Reiki self-healing treatment and my morning meditation.

> Just for today, I will not worry.
> Just for today, I will not get angry.
> Just for today, I will be honest.
> Just for today, I will be grateful.
> Just for today, I will love myself and every living thing.

I become much more aware of my emotions, and am starting to learn that they are something I can control. Anger is not really an issue for me, I hardly ever get angry. Worry, however, is a big one. I worry about pretty much everything! Has worry ever helped me solve a problem? No, on the contrary: worry makes my mind go round in endless circles that trap me in my own fear.

---

[4] See Further Reading List at the end of the book for references to book titles.

Simply repeating the precepts every day allows my focus to shift into a more positive mind-set. Every time I start to worry about something, I simply repeat over and over in my head 'Just for today, I will not worry.' After a while, I can feel my worry subside and my body goes back to being calm.

Exploring this new world of energy is certainly more fun than I have had in years. When the opportunity arises to take my learning further, I sign up for Reiki Level Two. I feel like a pioneer on an adventure to conquer new frontiers of existence as old as humankind. It's six months on from my first introduction to Reiki and I have a tool to dispel the darkness when it comes. Don't get me wrong, the darkness does still come, but now I am no longer helpless. I can recognise the signs, take time out, meditate, self-care and allow my inner light to shine through the darkness. The second Reiki level helps me go even deeper within. Not being able to speak is an absolute blessing, as I find connecting to the energy world much easier without all the distractions and noises of the physical world.

I learn, I practice, I meditate. The precepts become an integral part of my life and I feel so much more positive, despite the pain I'm still in. Reiki gives me hope. Hope that there is more than I currently know. Hope that in that 'more', I will one day find the solution that has so far eluded me. Hope that maybe, in this new world of quantum energy, healing exists as a possibility.

CHAPTER 8
THE TEMPEST

The December coldness seeps into my bones. Lifeless thorns tightly grip my womb. A friend and I have booked tickets for 'The Tempest'. I have my period, but I am so fed up with avoiding life and I do love Shakespeare, so I dose up on Paracetamol and Ibuprofen, determined to make it through a night at my favourite theatre. I fidget on my seat during the play. However much weight transferring I do, my bottom half is screaming to lie down in an Epsom salt bath or with a hot water bottle. I have reached a pain level during my periods now where no amount of conventional painkillers makes any difference. They only take the edge off a tiny bit.

On the stage in front of me, the play unfolds. Ariel speaks, "Hell is empty and all devils are here". I want to pass out and cannot wait for the interval. Luckily, my friend and I have gone in separate cars, so he stays, while I drive myself home. The pain is overwhelming. I decide not to risk the motorway, as exits often get blocked off at night for repair works. Every fibre of my being just wants to be home.

The country lane is pitch dark, rain is hammering on my windscreen. My driving is automated. I am elsewhere. It takes all my remaining strength to keep my eyes on the road. A wave of pain hits me. I am in my own tempest. My car goes into a bend way too fast and skids on the wet tarmac. I come up for air to see a tree looming in my path. I have no control anymore. Everything happens in slow motion. Time is suspended. The illuminated oak steps out from the darkness. Time stands still while a voice in my head says, "Just let go. If you let go now, it'll all be over." I am flooded with joy and an overwhelming sense of peace. This cosy, warm, pain free non-existence is calling me with the sweetest of siren songs.

> "We are such stuff
> As dreams are made on, and our little life
> Is rounded with a sleep."
> (Prospero's soliloquy in The Tempest, Act IV)

I am in another dimension. My son appears in front of my mind's eye. "Mummyyyyyy!" The sirens lose their hold and Jack's scream pulls me back into the car. I yank the steering wheel around, swerving onto the other side of the road as my car is doing a full circle around its own axis. The road is steeped in utter darkness, no other vehicles have ventured out on this wet and stormy winter night. I come to a stop. I'm slumped over the steering wheel in utter shock, white knuckles holding on for dear life. All I can hear is my own breathing. My whole body shakes. My heart is racing. I steer back onto the correct side of the road. It feels surreal. A split second that felt like an eternity. Relief. Fear. Joy. Regret. Jack. Phew… What just happened?

'Ok God, whatever you are and wherever you are, I just need to make something clear. I know I had these 'I don't want to live anymore' thoughts, but I didn't mean it! I'm not done yet.' F…ck! That was close. The joy and elation I felt at the thought of it all being over scares the hell out of me. Do optimists ever kill themselves? That night is the turning point. There is a very clear voice in my head saying: 'Enough! You have got to do something about this. You cannot carry on like this. Stop running away from the reality that endometriosis is winning and you are losing. Stop pretending you can just carry on with life as if everything is fine. It's not fine. Nothing is fine!' Tears well up. How did I get here? Why me?

That moment in the car is my wake-up call. Was God testing

how serious I was about ending it all? Was God showing me how beautiful death would be for my soul and giving me the option: carry on my journey on Earth or go back home? By choosing Jack's voice over that of the sirens, I had chosen life. But I also knew one hundred percent that if I chose life, I wanted to live and not just exist. Life is more than what I had been living over the past nine years of my slow decline into suffering and pain.

From that night onwards, the two voices in my head become more dominant: the victimised endo sufferer who sees no way out and the voice of resilience and hope are constantly arguing with each other. The endo voice is definitely the louder of the two and masks itself as the voice of reason. The voice of resilience and hope is starting out as nothing more than a shy little whisper, but its willpower is gaining strength.

> LITTLE VOICE: "Right. Enough is enough! You have got to stop this. There has got to be a way of fighting this illness. I DO NOT WANT TO DIE! I AM NOT READY TO DEPART THIS EARTH! UNDERSTOOD?"

> VOICE OF REASON: "Very funny. It's not like I haven't tried to get better. I read books, I read medical studies and articles. I changed my diet. I see homeopaths, iridologists, acupuncturists, nutritionists. Maybe it's time to admit defeat. Maybe I should have a hysterectomy. I mean, lots of other women seem to be fine after it. What if it did solve the problem? What if I didn't need HRT afterwards or would be absolutely fine on it. I'm not my mum. There is no proof I'd have the same problems she had when she went on HRT. Maybe it's time to stop being so stubborn. Maybe it's time to finally see sense."

LITTLE VOICE: "I'm not sure. It just doesn't' feel right."

VOICE OF REASON: "What do you mean, it doesn't feel right? What kind of argument is that? Dr. Myers said, she'd see me on her operating table sooner or later anyway. She said whatever I did, it wouldn't work long-term; it would just mask the truth, namely that the endometriosis is spreading silently inside me while I might feel I'm getting better. Well, I am in bloody pain almost every day now. So let's stop pretending! Endo is eating me up from the inside. Face the bloody truth: Dr. Myers was right. She was right all along and I've been a bloody fool."

LITTLE VOICE: "What if you haven't looked everywhere yet? What if there is something you've overlooked. Don't make any rash decisions. You can't think straight you're in that much pain. Please just give yourself a little more time. Go back on the internet. If you have a hysterectomy that's it. They can't put your womb back in once they've taken it out. Please just have one more look. If nothing comes up, fine. Then we'll have the hysterectomy. And if they've got to take part of the bowel out and even if you end up with a colostomy bag, it'll be ok. At least thanks to dad, you know what to expect, so there won't be any surprises. Just one more google search. Agreed?"

VOICE OF REASON: "Ok. One more search. That's it though!"

The google search brings up an endometriosis specialist in the north of England, whose name I can't pronounce. He seems to do an operation called peritoneal excision. I've never heard of it, but according to his website he has incredible results treating endometriosis and I would be able to keep all my organs. "Well, if you think he can help you, go and see him," my husband says.

I am thinking about the £350 consultation fee and all the money I've already spent on alternative methods that helped a bit, but didn't cure me. Given the pain I'm in right now, they seem to have been a wasted investment. I feel guilt and shame. My husband already knows that health has no price tag, a lesson I am still learning. It is a long way up north. Do I really want to go there? What if this so called endo specialist is a fraud? Surely if there was an operation that proved to have better results, my gynaecologist would have known about it and would have mentioned it?

Despite all my rational doubts, my gut is excited, proper butterfly excited. Thanks to my Reiki journey, I have learned to notice and listen to my gut feeling. I ring up to make an appointment and book my train ticket. The appointment is a month away. It feels like a glimmer of hope. One I'm almost too scared to look at for fear of yet another disappointment.

CHAPTER 9
A NEW DOOR OPENS

Ping. A What's App message on my phone. It's from my husband's cousin: "Just saw this article on endometriosis. Isn't that what you've got? Thought it might be interesting." I follow the link in the message. It takes me to an article that connects endometriosis and cancer via something called Warburg effect. Scientists have discovered that endometriosis seems to start with the same cell changes that happen in cancer cells. The behaviour of the effected cells is very similar. This reminds me of my gynaecologist who had once used the same analogy when describing endometriosis to me very early on, saying the way that endometriosis progressed and presented in the body was very similar to cancer, just that it wouldn't kill me.

I research Warburg effect and the name Dr. Johanna Budwig keeps popping into my head. Who is Dr. Budwig? She was a German biochemist and cell researcher who devoted her life to cancer research and wrote many papers and books on cell changes in cancer cells and how these could be reversed naturally. As a renowned German scientist in the 1950s and 60s, she was very aware of Otto Warburg's work from the 1920s. Both of them were trailblazers in their fields. Otto Warburg was awarded a Nobel Prize in physiology in 1931. Dr. Johanna Budwig was nominated for several Nobel Prizes during her life time.

I know about Dr. Budwig from the time my dad had stage IV bowel cancer. At the time, I had read a lot of her books and articles to help my dad. I remember being in absolute awe of her work. I very clearly remember thinking back then: I would love to go to a

Budwig Centre and learn all about this, but without the 'having cancer bit'. Her approach made such sense to me, and I do believe her protocol helped my father survive his cancer.

If the research paper my husband's cousin has just sent me is correct, Warburg effect cell changes are the very first stage of endometriosis.[5] If Budwig's cancer protocol works at cell level, reversing these Warburg effect cell changes, then her approach should theoretically work for endometriosis.

I ring my mum and ask if she still has the Budwig books[6] we read ten years ago. I can't really remember any details about her protocol. We have a chat about what exactly my dad did. I google the centre in Germany that treats people according to the Budwig protocol. It's called the 3E Centre[7]. Their whole approach focuses on three areas of wellbeing: nutrition (Ernährung), detoxification (Entgiftung) and energy work (Energiearbeit). In German, these three main pillars of healing all start with the letter E, hence the name 3E Centre.

I receive a reply within days. While they do treat people with other illnesses, 95% of their patients have cancer and they've never knowingly treated anyone with endometriosis, so they couldn't say if their programme would work. If I did decide to book on the programme, it would be a four week residential stay at the centre, costing almost ten thousand Euros. My heart sinks. My two voices are back. In my mind, they are like two actors on a stage, and I am the observer of their play.

VOICE OF REASON [paces around the room]:
"There is no way I can spend that much money

---

[5] Vicky J Young, Jeremy K Brown et al: Transforming growth factor-β induced Warburg-like metabolic reprogramming may underpin the development of peritoneal endometriosis. The Journal of Clinical endocrinology and metabolism. September 2014.
[6] See Further Reading List at the end of the book for bookt titles in English.
[7] www.3Ecentre.com

on myself. Forget it. It's too expensive. And it may not even work. They've never treated anyone with endometriosis."

LITTLE VOICE [skips around enthusiastically, like a young child]: "What if it works though... I feel really excited... I think this is it... this might be what we've been waiting for..."

VOICE OF REASON [interrupting]: "... you and your gut feeling. It's ridiculous. How are you going to justify spending that much money? And besides, it's a whole month in Germany. How is that going to work? I can't just disappear for a month! What about the family? Who is going to do the school runs? Who is going to cook dinners? Jack needs his mum. And who will walk the dog? It's not possible."

Little voice does something it has never done before. It carries on speaking.

LITTLE VOICE [hesitantly with quiet courage]: "But we could perhaps, just talk to David about it, couldn't we?... After all, what have we got to lose?... We can't carry on as we are, existing, not living."

VOICE OF REASON [taking back control again]: "No. We've got the appointment with the endometriosis specialist up north. Let's see what comes of that and then make a decision."

LITTLE VOICE [breaking new ground by speaking again]: "... but would it be ok if we started the Budwig diet now? That way we can see if it does anything or not. It may not work anyway. But I'd love to give it a go."

VOICE OF REASON [nods their head].

[Little voice jumps for joy. It may not have been fully heard, but it had the courage to speak up.]

I find lots of information online and order several of Dr. Johanna Budwig's books[8], which I start reading immediately. The main thing seems to be cutting out any animal protein and sugar. I prefer vegetarian food anyway and we only eat a little chicken and fish occasionally, so I can't see this being a problem. The second important thing is eating the 'Budwig Cream' every day, a hundred grams for breakfast and a hundred grams for lunch. This is a mixture of quark (similar to cottage cheese, which is naturally fat free and high in protein) and linseed oil. Here we go, let another guinea pig experiment begin!

There is no rational explanation for how elated I feel. After all, I have no idea if this will work. But I feel an excitement inside that I haven't felt since learning Reiki. Hope, an inner knowing… whatever it is, I like it.

---

[8] Dr. Johanna Budwig: Flax Oil as a True Aid Against Arthritis, Heart Infarction and Cancer. Apple Publishing, 1994. (Add Publisher and year) Dr Johanna Budwig: Oel-Eiweiss Kost. Sensei, 2013.
A good English website about the protocol is www.budwig-diet.co.uk

CHAPTER 10
DECISION TIME: SURGERY OR GERMANY

On a cold day in February, five hours after leaving home, two trains, a bus ride and a one mile walk later, I find myself sitting opposite an endometriosis specialist understands my illness better than anyone I've ever met. For a hefty consultation fee, he spends ninety minutes with me, meticulously explaining endometriosis and why he thinks the conventional approaches of hysterectomy or lasering only bring short term relief, but are no long-term solution.

We look at images, he draws and sketches. Everything he says makes total sense. He shows me statistics, success rates that should be called failure rates: 65% of endo related hysterectomy patients experience symptoms again within two to three years.

He then explains, what he does instead. He was one of the first British surgeons to introduce an operation called peritoneal excision in the UK, a procedure developed by a German surgeon in the 1990s. He explains that this excision surgery would be removing the first layer of skin from the inside. This skin layer is called the peritoneum and is a membrane that lines the abdominal cavity, including the intro-abdominal organs. The peritoneum contains the endometriosis tissue.

By practically skinning me from the inside, there is a much better chance of removing all the endometriosis cells, including those a surgeon cannot yet see that are already implanted. It is a time consuming operation, as the surgeon has to be incredibly precise and careful, removing this skin layer off the major organs like the bowel, which can be risky if not done by an excision expert.

He looks at my latest MRI scan and all my reports, "You know, we divide endometriosis into four stages of severity: stage I, II, III and IV. You have stage IV, the worst stage we diagnose. Now imagine a scale of one to ten for just the stage IV endometriosis patients, with one being a mild stage IV and ten being the worst case scenario. On that scale, you would be a ten." I'm not too shocked, but it does bring home just how ill I clearly am. I knew I was in a bad state, even though I had tried desperately to not face the truth. It dawns on me that getting this healed will be no walk in the park.

He explains that because of the severity of my case, two operations would be necessary. The first one would take about five to six hours and would excise the ovaries and uterus, which have completely fused together with the endometriosis tissue. The second operation would be a month or so later and would last about ten hours, excising the rest of my peritoneum. He has retired from the NHS[9], so only operates privately and the cost for both operations together would be around thirty five thousand pounds. My heart drops. I finally thought I'd found a surgery option I'd be willing to explore, but the price tag is a hefty one. If I opt for excision, I want him to do it, I totally trust him.

> "You know, this operation is being done elsewhere, too." I hear him say, while my mind is thinking about how I could pay for this. "I am not the only surgeon doing this operation. There are Endometriosis Centres all over the country that often offer this type of surgery. It's usually done by a team of surgeons rather than just one

---

[9] NHS stands for National Health Service and is the state funded British healthcare provider.

> person, which means less time under anaesthetic. Traditionally, there would be a gynaecological surgeon, a bowel surgeon and an urologist working together, each dealing with their area of expertise. It just so happens that I do all of it myself, and because of that you would need two operations, as I cannot concentrate for 15 hours at the level of precision required."

I'm completely flabbergasted that there are Endometriosis Centres all over the country. How did I not know this? Does he mean to say there might be a specialist centre near where I live?

> "Yes, I am sure there is one near you. So you might want to have a look at your options first. I'm a long way away from your home. Don't make any rash decisions, do some research first."

He is so genuine and so honestly interested in my welfare, I would like to wrap him up and take him home with me. I thank him and leaving his office, I feel a little more positive. Peritoneal excision surgery makes more sense to me than a hysterectomy and it seems to have better long-term success rates.

On the train home, I mull over everything I have learned. I cannot believe that neither my general practitioner nor my gynaecologist have ever mentioned the existence of Endometriosis Centres. A quick online search reveals there is an Endometriosis Clinic about 30 minutes from where I live and the excision specialist there trained in Germany under the surgeon who developed peritoneal excision in the first place. How were my doctors and gynaecologists not aware of this? Maybe because the clinic is private, which probably explains why nobody in the NHS system has ever mentioned this. Although, I still believe they should. I'm a big believer in making informed decisions and looking at all my options. Excision surgery doesn't seem to be readily available on the NHS. There are, however, hospitals even on the NHS that have excision specialists.

When I get back home, I immediately make an appointment at the Endometriosis Clinic near me. How did I not find this before?

It is February. My appointment at the Endometriosis Clinic is in April. I am in my kitchen, putting quark and linseed oil onto the fridge shelf. Johanna Budwig's books are lying on the work surface. The shelves have been reorganised and are now stocked with seeds and nuts. The fridge is bursting with fresh fruit and vegetables. I cannot ignore the voice inside me that wants to try Budwig's approach before agreeing to surgery. I have to try. It's my last straw.

Excision surgery would cost three times more than it would cost to go to the Budwig Clinic in Germany. The fee for the German clinic would definitely have to come out of my pocket. Could I go? During March, my mind rattles away constantly weighing up my options. Even if my private health insurance did pay (which is unlikely), would I rather have surgery than try yet another alternative approach? There is a cost attached to both paths. I decide that whether I pay myself or not should not influence my decision making process. A purely financial approach cannot be the right way of looking at this. The Budwig path is cheaper, and most importantly my gut resonates more with this option.

Surgery always carries risks. The Budwig approach has no side effects whatsoever. I would love to at least try Germany. But what if the Budwig cancer protocol doesn't work? Excision surgery seems to have really good results. The experts at the 3E Centre have never had a patient with endometriosis. They treat cancer patients. I am completely relying on the study that links cancer and endometriosis via the Warburg effect. It's a massive risk: a total experiment. On the other hand, if it doesn't work, the option of surgery is always there later. I don't know what to do. Day after day, I'm debating my options, going round in circles. It still feels extremely uncomfortable to me to justify spending this sort of money on my health.

It's April. My mum phones. My parents split up after forty five years of marriage. My mum sold our family home and both my parents have downsized. I cannot believe the words that I hear through the receiver:

> "Well, I was thinking that instead of you and your brother inheriting whatever I have when I am dead, I would like to give you both fifteen thousand Euros now. After all, I won't need all the money from the house sale, I get a good pension. This way, I can at least enjoy watching you spend it. What is the point of waiting till I am dead?"

A faint light of hope ignites, the break of dawn, a first shimmer of light that ushers in a new day.

"Wow... are you sure?"

> I'm getting super excited! This is the sign I've been waiting for. The universe is telling me what to do. The money is not enough for excision surgery, but it's more than enough for Germany.

"Mum. Would you mind if I used the money to go to the Budwig Centre? I would really love to try and see if this Budwig protocol works for my endometriosis... I just have this feeling it might. I cannot explain why. I would totally be taking a risk. But I get this really excited feeling in my tummy when I think of going there."

"Darling, it's your money. I will put it into your account this week and then it's up to you what you do with it. If I know it helps you, what better present could there be for me than to watch you heal."

"Oh mum, I love you! Thank you! Thank you! Thank you!"

"You know, if you do go to Germany for a month, I can come and look after Jack and David. You know: cook for them, do the washing. If it helps..."

"Oh mum, that would be just amazing! Let me ring the 3E Centre and find out how it would work."

I end the call and feel elated. I ring the centre immediately, my heart is beating fast. The month of May is fully booked but they have a space in their June intake. This actually works perfectly as it gives me almost six weeks to organise everything at home, and to book flights for me and my mum. I am super excited!

Might this be the answer I have been looking for? Might this truly finally be the new dawn after all those long hours of darkness? When my April appointment at the endometriosis clinic comes along, I decide to still go. It can't hurt to meet the consultant there, see what experience he has and whether excision surgery with him might be another option. I come away feeling that this could be a possible plan B. The consultant trained in Germany. He seems to know what he is doing and would operate with a team of three other surgeons, a bowel specialist, a bladder specialist and the gynaecologist would each focus on their area of expertise. It would be just one operation. My voice of reason feels reassured. It can see that plan B will work and this knowledge makes it feel safe and willing to agree to plan A.

I tell the consultant about my plan to go to Germany and try the Budwig approach first. We agree that should this not work, I would get back to him to arrange excision surgery. The dietary changes I started to make in February are already starting to have a positive effect. I'm less constipated, less bloated and have a little more energy, even though the pain is still bad for almost two weeks every month. I am looking at a horizon filled with light and hope, instead of looking at a black chasm of impenetrable darkness and pain. My body turns east towards Germany. East is always where the new dawn rises.

CHAPTER 11
THE 3E CENTRE

The time for my departure has arrived. A month away from my family, my son… excitement mixes with a little apprehension. Is this the right decision? Is this going to finally heal me? Am I wasting a lot of money? Are these people charlatans?

I go into the airport bookshop and a novel catches my eye. I tell myself that under no circumstances will I buy another book. Having studied English, French and Russian literature, my house is covered in books. I am aimlessly scanning the shelves, when the orange cover of a book draws me in. I walk out. I am not buying a book. Of course, I return to just find out what book it is. It's called *The Alchemist* by Paolo Coelho.

On the plane, my head is buried in The Alchemist. I am not reading, my mind is rattling away, wondering what the journey will bring. A man sits down on the seat next to me.

"It's a really good book."

"Oh. Do you know it? I just bought it at the airport."

"Yes, I read it years ago."

"I dream of writing a book one day."

I have never spoken those words aloud. Not to anyone. Where did that come from? How did I just confide my biggest dream to a total stranger? Until now, I hadn't even dared to fully, openly admit my wish to one day be an author to myself. Maybe I feel safe precisely because he is a stranger? If I never write a book, it's fine. He wouldn't be able to ring me up and go, 'Have you written it yet?' No pressure. It feels big to finally say it out loud.

I have known my whole life I would one day write a book. When I was 18, a thought popped into my head: 'Before I can write a book, I have to ruin my life first. Only then will I have something to write about.' It was such a random thought. It just materialized out of nowhere, but it stuck in my head ever since. For years and years, I looked at my perfect life, frustrated that it wasn't book worthy.

I wanted to write all my life. As a child, I would spend hours reading books, stories, fairy tales. Whenever anyone was looking for me, they would find me with a book: in a chair, on the sofa, leaning against a tree in the garden, or in winter often on top of my wardrobe, where I had made myself a little den. The wardrobe stood next to a chimney and I would lean my back against the warm bricks, snuggled up in cushions and blankets. My best friend and I would write stories together in little note books, inventing characters, sending them on adventures. It dawned on me sitting on that plane, that maybe I had ruined my life enough now to finally write?

"Make sure you write about something you have experienced yourself," I hear the man next to me say, "That's when your writing will be authentic." We have a good little chat, philosophising about the meaning of life, and in no time the plane touches down on the runway in Germany. It is one of those brief little gem human encounters that happen in life.

The taxi from the airport soon winds its way out of human urbanisation and I find myself surrounded by fields, orchards and forests. The region is famous for its rolling hills, small sleepy villages and towns, peaceful rural atmosphere, none of which I am taking in, because I'm so nervous about what is to come. I am not just leaving civilization, people, airports, train stations, bus stops, shops and restaurants behind, but my home, my family and the life I have known. This is going to be a month of just me. I have no idea what to expect. I hope for nothing, and everything.

I feel the fear of the unknown mingling with a sense of excitement in my stomach. Deep down I know, this is my chance. My chance to find myself again. It feels like I lost myself somewhere along the journey of my life and I have come in search of myself. The taxi pulls up outside a white building. It doesn't look like a clinic, more like a seminar centre. Bubbles in my tummy, my heart skipping, I hold my breath and stand alone outside the front entrance. Who will spend the month with me? I know that there is going to be a group of us. A group of strangers, spending a month together, away from their normal lives, to find themselves. To heal. While I am healing from endometriosis, the others are most likely healing from cancer. I have no idea how ill the other people are going to be and part of me feels like a fraud. I don't have the big C, my illness affects every day of my life, but it isn't life-threatening. I do not have to be scared or worried that endometriosis might kill me. Every cloud has a silver lining. A month seems such a long time.

I ring the bell, and wait. A woman opens and welcomes me warmly. I'm too nervous to notice what she is wearing. She walks me to my room. The building is clean but sparse. The empty corridors feel very friendly, full of heart. There is beautiful art work on the walls everywhere, which is soothing. A painting of an Indian chief in full headdress straight away speaks to my heart. I used to love playing cowboys and Indians as a child, and while most of the other children wanted to be the cowboys, I always chose to be the Indian. There is a piano on the first floor. Big open windows look out over countryside and forest. We are all going to meet at six o'clock, for a welcome drink and dinner.

My room is on the ground floor, with patio doors leading out onto a little terrace. I look out of the window and all I see is green. Balsam for my soul. A meadow in front of my terrace is calling my tired feet, I walk out to find a beautiful garden with a pond to my right, frogs croaking. I raise my head and my eyes feast on the ancient forest. My heart sings. This is the perfect place to find myself. I am a forest girl. My father is a hunter and I spent my childhood in the forest. I am never happier than when I am roaming amongst the trees, bushes and greenery, breathing in the musty scent of leaves and wood composting on the forest floor, birds singing in the canopy above. I inhale deeply and almost sigh with pleasure: I am home.

CHAPTER 12
ASSESSMENT WEEK

The first week is an assessment week. We all get to settle into our new life, our new surroundings that are to be home for the next month. We also get assessed by the centre's medical staff, to ensure we are all fit enough for the programme. Last month, the centre was filled to full capacity with seventeen patients plus their partners (you have the option of bringing your partner). This month, there is only six of us and we have all come alone. This will turn out to be a real treat. Being such a small group will mean we really bond and get to know each other in a way that just would not have happened, had there been seventeen of us.

We will spend four life-changing weeks together. Each one of us is on their own journey. Each one desperately trying to stay here on Earth a bit longer, beat whatever illness we have in order to live life. How will this month change us? The centre tells us this is a shifting point in our lives. We will forever be looking at life as before and after our month here. How will our new life differ from the one we left behind, the old life, in which we still took health for granted?

None of us knows what the others have or why any of us are here. The 3E Centre does not allow us to talk about our illnesses. We are to meet each other as humans, not as illnesses or labels. Despite this, I find myself guessing. What is it about being human that makes us want to categorise and label? Six people, six stories, six journeys thrown together for four weeks. Four weeks that will change our lives forever. Four weeks of burning our old selves, so our true selves can rise like a phoenix from the ashes.

I partly feared the 3E Centre was another money-making machine, where cancer keeps the till ringing. Before I arrived, €408 a day seemed a hefty sum to pay for a room without TV or internet. By the time I leave, I will think it's an absolute bargain. I hadn't expected the staff to spend the first week assessing whether their approach might work for me or not. I am even more surprised that I will be sent home with a full refund, if the assessors don't think the Budwig approach might help me. During the first week, we all have an appointment with the centre's resident healing practitioner and cancer advisor, another with a doctor and a third with a specialist in dark field microscopy.

Dark field microscopy is absolutely fascinating. I cannot believe I've never heard of it and it doesn't get used by every doctor in the world to establish what's wrong with a patient. The actual apparatus doesn't look that different from a normal microscope and the dark field part refers to the way the image is produced, which leaves a dark field around the specimen being looked at. A little prick in your finger draws one drop of blood, which is put on a petri dish and observed under the dark field microscope. Red and white blood cells, T-marker cells, proteins all become visible.

There is a whole world inside one single drop of my blood! My red cells are all shrivelled up, apparently a sign of dehydration (I am awful at drinking my 2 litres a day!). My white blood cells and my T-cells are looking good, indicating a healthy immune system. This surprises me, as I always thought my immune system must be weak to not be able to fight endometriosis. According to the microscope however, my problem is not a weak immune system. There is a snowstorm raging under the microscope and I learn that all those snowflake dots busily dashing about are proteins. Quite a considerable amount of them are clustered together to form crystal like shapes. I can see other little cells nibbling away at the crystals, trying to break them up. I learn that snowflakes are better than crystals. The crystal formations indicate that there are too many toxins and fungi in the body, putting a strain on my system. Due to the sheer volume, the white blood cells and T-cells are unable to eliminate the toxic load efficiently.

Another mind-blowing test reveals that my liver isn't working optimally. As the liver is our main detox organ, it makes sense that my body is overloaded with toxins. The test I have to do to find this out is super simple: I drink a shot glass of an alkaline solution. Depending on my body's deficiency, the taste of the solution I drink will vary, giving the medical staff an indication of what is amiss within me. If it tastes salty, there is an issue with my connective tissue or muscles. If it tastes bitter or metallic, my kidneys are the problem. A fishy taste - as is the case with me - means the liver is not working properly. A rotten egg taste means gall bladder problems. A sweet taste indicates issues in the endocrine system and the pancreas. Sour, chlorine taste means stomach issues. A sharp, burning sensation indicates poor blood circulation and heart problems.

It's a shot glass of a drink! How much money do we spend on MRI scans, ultrasounds and all sorts of tests when a single shot of alkaline solution can tell us this much about our body? Can this be real? Fast forward and I will do this test again and again at home, using a glass of water with a little bicarbonate of soda, which works almost as well, even though the taste is less intense. In the months after my stay here, this test will give me an indication on my toxin levels.

I pass all the tests, which means I'm well enough to stay. They do make it clear again, that they have never treated anyone with endometriosis. I trust my gut and the study paper linking endo cells and cancer cells. Everything I have learned and experienced seems to make total sense, at least to me. Based on the tests, my medical records and assessments, the month's programme gets designed for my individual needs. The Centre has a PAPIMI machine, which everyone gets to use every day. The PAPIMI device creates a pulsed electromagnetic field which can be applied to different parts of the body. The idea is that it helps to stimulate and activate the normal healing process, including the growth and repair of tissue. It raises the energy levels in the cells using specific frequency waves. Dr. Johanna Budwig's approach was all about raising the energy in the cells. Cancer cells vibrate at a low frequency, healthy cells vibrate at a high frequency. The aim is to raise the energy in the cells. A healthy cell will heal itself, so to speak.

In addition to the daily seminars and a whole variety of treatments included in the programme, there are optional extras. I choose to have Vitamin C infusions, and an immune boosting supplement made up of various spices, including turmeric.

We don't all pass the first week assessment. The cancer of one of our little group's patients is so advanced, that the assessors recommend an urgent round of chemotherapy. There is a clinic in Germany that actually does what they call localised chemotherapy. The chemo drugs are fed only into the tumour and filtered out of the blood stream the minute they exit the tumour. This means, only the cancer cells are killed, the rest of the body which is healthy can function normally. It's an amazing treatment, but not offered in the mainstream healthcare system. It is much cheaper than conventional chemotherapy, as you need a smaller amount of the drug and there are hardly any side effects. To the patient, however, it's more expensive, as it is only offered privately, no health insurance will pay.

Unless our fellow group member does either a localised or conventional round of chemotherapy, he will not have the time he would need for Budwig's approach to work. It takes two to three months for healing to start under her protocol. He does not have that time. He has, however, had chemotherapy before and refuses to have it again. The memory is making him shiver. He would rather die. A few days later he is too weak to come out of his room. His wife comes to pick him up and we learn a week later that he passed away.

It's a sobering experience for all of us. The choices we make are choices of life and death. This may be a scarier realisation for the others than for me: I know endometriosis will not kill me. Still, a little doubt creeps in: was it the right choice to come here? To go against normal school medicine? To try a natural, alternative, holistic approach to healing? Our little team of fighters is down to five.

CHAPTER 13

THE WARBURG EFFECT & BUDWIG'S FINDINGS

Dr. Johanna Budwig started her career researching fats, when working for the German government. She was an incredible woman and pioneer in her field. Nominated for several Nobel prizes for her work on fats and the human cell, she eventually discovered what turned a healthy cell into a cancer cell: bad fats. The cell membranes of our cells are made up of fatty acids. The cell communicates via protein bridges with the body, telling the body what it needs. Protein carriers working with a key lock system supply the cell with all the nutrients, enzymes, hormones and all things it needs to function. Only the protein with the right key will be able to pass through the fat membrane.

Most things our cells need, such as nutrients or enzymes, are water soluble. Anyone who ever poured oil and water into a glass will know that the two don't mix. The oil will stay on top of the water, creating a clear cut barrier. The inside of a cell is made up of water, the outside environment of a cell is water based and the fat membrane forms an impermeable fatty coating that gives the cell control over what is allowed in or is not allowed in. It separates the inside from the outside. Nothing can penetrate this membrane, unless the cell's gatekeepers bring it in. There are hundreds of different types of proteins carrying things in and out of the cell across the fat membrane. I think of them as little Sherpa carriers, the men of the Tibetan ethnic group that carry all the provisions for hikers going up and down Mount Everest. The cell, membrane and proteins all communicate with each other, keeping the cell nourished and thriving. In cancer cells, this protein communication breaks down, practically starving the cell of what it needs.

The cell membrane is made up of building blocks of fatty acids, fat blocks. These blocks get renewed constantly. Imagine a house where the bricks that form its outer walls are continuously swapped and renewed. The fats used for this are supplied by the body, absorbed from our food. There is just one problem: there are good and bad fats in this world. The good fats speak the language of the proteins, the bad fats don't.

The modern Western diet is full of bad fats from processed foods. Most fats change their structure and become trans fats when we heat them up. And most processed foods we buy, such as ready meals, cakes, biscuits, crackers, potato crisps or chips use oil that has been heated (pasteurized or hydrogenated). Just like the heat of boiling or frying at a high temperature would kill our life force, it is killing the life force contained in a cold pressed oil. The oil that was alive and full of healthy fats is now dead, but able to stand on a supermarket shelf for months without going off. A cold pressed oil that hasn't been heated, such as an extra virgin olive oil, would be an example of a good fat. Good fats are alive and transfer electromagnetic currents, which is how they communicate with the proteins.

The body cannot distinguish between a good and a bad fat, it uses whatever fat is available through our diet to keep those fatty cell membranes intact. Bad fats now become the building blocks for our cell membrane, but as we have learned, they don't speak the language of the proteins: the cell can no longer communicate with its gatekeepers, its food supply chain stops and the cell starves. No oxygen gets into the cell anymore, it's a cell lockdown.

In a desperate attempt to survive, the cell starts creating energy through a fermentation process. This is what is called the Warburg effect. The cell becomes an island unto itself, and is effectively disconnected from the body's system. There is no communication with the rest of the body. These cells become underground networks that remain undetected by the immune system that would usually eliminate them. They also no longer behave like a healthy cell which would split and die at the end of its life cycle. These cells are like a zombie in a horror movie: they split and live - a growing tumour not playing by the rules of nature.

Budwig believed that anything the body had created, the body could un-create, or correct. Would it be possible to reverse this lockdown process? What would need to be done to repair the communication channels? The cell membrane constantly renews itself, replacing old building blocks of fat with new ones. If we supply the body with good naturally occurring cold pressed fats instead of the processed fats that caused the membrane to malfunction, could the cell be restored back to health? Budwig established, that this was indeed the case and that it was possible to repair the cell and to reconnect it to the body's communication system.

When it comes to cancer, we are often in a race against time. So the next question was how we could get good fats and proteins into the body quickly in order to restore the fat protein communication. Budwig found that the best combination of fatty acids in the ratio needed by the human cell naturally occurred in linseed or flaxseed oil. A source of protein easily available in 1950s and 1960s Germany was quark, a by-product of milk production. Quark is high in protein and naturally fat free. After intensive research, Budwig decided that mixing high protein quark with linseed oil was the easiest way of providing what was needed to restore the cell. The famous Budwig Crème was born.

In her research, Budwig also found that the body metabolised plant based fats and plant based protein much easier than animal fats and animal protein. Let's imagine the body as an energy system, controlled by energy input and output. We eat in order to absorb the energy contained in the food: energy that plants have absorbed from the soil, water and sunshine; or energy that animals have absorbed through eating plants or other animals that have eaten plants. Digestion is the process that allows us to do this, but this process requires a certain amount of energy in itself. The less energy we need for the digestive process, and the higher the energy content of the food we eat, the more energy is available in the body to live life. From an energy perspective, digesting meat or fish takes a lot more energy than digesting fruits and vegetables. Budwig came to the conclusion in the 1950s, that all animal fats and animal proteins should be eliminated from the diet, giving the body a better chance of creating surplus energy reserves that could be used for cell renewal and restoration.

Looking at cells under a microscope for most of her research life, she also noticed that health was order and structure, symmetry and beauty, while illness or disease was chaos and disorder. To get any disease under control and to get the body back to health, structure and order had to be re-established in all aspects of life. She designed a whole daily routine that the 3E Centre follows meticulously. This is known as the Budwig Protocol, often referred to as the Budwig Diet. It is much more than a diet, however, it's a way of life. The three main pillars Budwig's protocol rests on are nutrition, detoxification and energy work. In German, the words for these three pillars all start with the letter E, hence the centre is called the 3E Centre. In essence, the program is all about:

E1 = Ernährung (nutrition): not putting anything bad or processed into the body's system and eating healthily;

E2 = Entgiftung (detoxification): helping the body eliminate the toxins in the system as efficiently as possible;

E3 = Energiearbeit (energy work): raising the vibrations in the cells through positive thinking, reducing stress and working through emotional obstacles.

Every single human cell vibrates at a certain energy frequency, which can be measured. We are told in one of our lectures that the energy in a diseased cell vibrates at a much lower frequency than the energy in a healthy cell. Raising the energy in the cells is one of the main goals of Budwig's healing approach. Based on almost twenty years of their own experiences of working with cancer patients, the Centre reckons that 20 percent of success is linked to detox and nutrition, a whopping 80 percent is down to energy work and stress management.

For our little group of five, learning mindfulness and becoming aware of negative emotional patterns that cause us stress is going to be the main work over the next four weeks. It sounds so easy and simple, yet shall prove to be one of the hardest things to accomplish.

Our weekly schedule is a good balance of seminars and free time for self-reflection. We all have sessions with a life coach in addition to sessions with the holistic healing practitioner who has specialist cancer training.[10] Every morning there are seminars and workshops: meditation, mindfulness, positive thinking, breathing techniques as well as theory lectures on Budwig, fats, nutrition and energy. Afternoons are either free or filled with optional activities such as laughing yoga (one of our favourites!), mantra singing, massages, Tui Na, colon hydro therapy and plenty of time for forest walks.

As my mind learns to quieten down, there is suddenly space for observing my own journey. With each day, it becomes a little clearer, how and why I went down the wrong path in my life, the path that lead me here. Self-sacrifice, lack of self-love, not listening to my body and ignoring my own needs - taking responsibility for making the wrong choices and realising that certain decisions I made created the illness I now suffer from is the toughest part of

---

[10] In Germany, there is a specific training pathway to become a holistic cancer practitioner (Krebsberater).

the process. But oddly, it's also the most liberating. If I open up to the possibility that I played a part in creating the life that made me ill, then consequently I also have the power to create a life that makes me healthy again.

CHAPTER 14
EMBRACING A BUDWIG DAY

As I mentioned earlier, Budwig's approach aims to create order and structure. I soon get used to my new routine. It is really nice to only have to think about myself, to get my meals cooked and prepared and it's also oddly comforting to have a strict schedule to my day. In my new life, my day starts at 7am, when we all make our way into the dining room, where bottles of sunflower oil and sauerkraut juice are waiting.

The sunflower oil is for oil pulling. One tablespoon of oil gets, swished around the mouth for about 15 minutes, like you would do with a mouth wash. It takes a little getting used to and I gag the first few days. A whole tablespoon of oil in my mouth is not a sensation I'm used to. By day three, however, walking in the garden among the lavender bushes, watching the bees while I'm swishing, I've become a pro. They warned us on day one that spitting the oil down the sink afterwards would block the drains. So after 15 minutes, when the oil has absorbed all toxins and nasty bacteria from my mouth and become white, I spit it into a little paper cup with kitchen roll. Apparently spitting it into the garden will kill the plants after a while.

Talking about blocked drains: another one of Budwig's remedies to increase the energy in the cells is to rub electron differentiating oils (ELDI oils) all over your body. They can be bought on the internet, or you can make your own by mixing wheat germ oil and linseed oil in equal amounts.

Oil pulling is followed by sauerkraut juice. As a German, I have grown up with Sauerkraut. It is naturally fermented white cabbage. My grandmother always had a large, knee high clay pot in the cellar of homemade Sauerkraut. While some people find the taste utterly disgusting, I absolutely love it and drinking 100ml of organic sauerkraut juice on an empty stomach every morning is not a problem for me.

After the first morning, nobody bothers getting dressed for our start to the day and we all just turn up in our pyjamas and dressing gowns. The first two steps of our daily routine completed, I go back to my room to do some yoga stretches, shower and get dressed in time for breakfast at 8. Breakfast is Budwig's quark crème, nuts, seeds, milled linseeds and a variety of fresh fruit. For those still hungry, there is buckwheat porridge. To drink, there is a selection of herbal teas.

The food is generally amazing! There are two chefs, turning organic vegetables into the most delicious, nutritious Budwig meals. One of them, Michael, is East German like me and when he speaks my heart warms instantly. Listening to him and observing my emotional reaction to his regional accent makes me realise how much I miss my old home. Not just the country or the culture, but the people. Given our shared heritage, it's not a surprise that we get on like a house on fire. There is a warmth, authenticity, openness and directness in him that I cherish. We have the same sense of humour, the same sharp, brutally honest wit with which we laugh about ourselves.

Michael used to work as a chef in a big upmarket hotel chain before he decided that working all hours was not what he wanted in life and was not in alignment with his values. At the 3E Centre, he can use his passion for food and for creating the most magical dishes in an environment of peace and calm to help people heal. He now shines his light by showing people that eating a healthy, vegetarian diet can be fun, creative, diverse and interesting. And let me tell you: the food is divine! And presented like a piece of art.

Coffee is not allowed, at least not absorbed orally. There is, however, a table with six thermos flasks of black coffee neatly lined up each morning. These are for our daily coffee enemas. Instead of letting it flow into our mouths, we let in flow into our backside. On day one we are all given an enema kit (kind of a bucket with a pipe and nozzle) and some Vaseline. The resident cancer practitioner Elsa explains what we need to do and we all have a slightly embarrassed self-conscious giggle. Each bathroom has a little bench covered with a rubber mat and a hook above it to hang the enema bucket.

I soon learn that when doing an enema you want to be close to the toilet and you need to have the bucket slightly above wherever your bum is, so gravity can help the coffee go where you want it. Trying to hold coffee inside your backside for 15 minutes, resisting the urge to 'go' takes a little practice. Imagine trying to hold diarrhoea. If you are not careful, the whole coffee poo mixture shoots out of you with the force of a rocket. Unstoppable! I promise you: you want to be as close to the toilet as you can be!

Coffee enemas stimulate the liver. In particular with cancer or chronic illnesses the liver tends to have become sluggish and doesn't work as well as it should. This means toxins stay in the body rather than getting removed. An overload of toxins means the liver is overworked and tired. Just like coffee has an energising effect on us, waking us up in the morning or in that lunchtime energy dip, taken as an enema it stimulates the liver. Together with the skin and bowel, the liver is one of our body's main detoxification organs, keeping our body system clean and tidy.

At 9.15am there are seminars or lectures every morning, usually for a couple of hours. There is then an individual schedule of doctors, life coach appointments, Papimi machine appointments (see glossary) and workshops. At 12.30 lunch gets served, a three course meal consisting of a salad buffet, a vegetarian main course and a Budwig crème dessert.

We have to go for a fifteen minute walk after each meal, to

help the digestive process. Either just before or after lunch, I do my daily coffee enema. I learn fairly quickly I have to do it before 2pm. Any later and I cannot sleep at night. It affects me like drinking a cup of coffee would.

At 6pm it's dinner, usually a light meal, such as vegetable soup or vegetarian rice. Most meals contain buckwheat. It's high in protein and it helps to bind and eliminate toxins from the digestive tract. At 10am and at 3pm we all get a fresh juice: carrot, apple, beetroot and ginger in the morning, while the afternoon juice is papaya, which apparently contains some powerful enzymes.

However filled the day may seem, there is plenty of time for 'me'. Too much time. The first week, I'm restless and don't know what to do with myself. I am so used to rushing around from the minute I get up in the morning to the minute my head hits the pillow at night, all this peace and quiet feels too much.

Experiencing what my body feels like when it is not stressed makes me realise just how stressful my average day at home actually is, how little I stop to breathe and relax. I almost never just sit and do nothing. At home, everything I do has a purpose, a walk isn't a walk for me, it's a walk for the dog to have a poo. And while I'm walking I'm usually thinking of all the things waiting to be done afterwards. Here, there are many minutes of nothing in my day, and all my minutes are mine. I have nothing to do for anyone other than myself. There is no internet, no TV. My mobile only works on top of the mountain, about a ten minute walk through a field.

Slowly, day after day, I get more used to this new pace of life. I read, I draw, I sit and watch ants crawling up a tree trunk, I walk, I watch the sunset. There are hunting stands all around the forest. I often go at dusk and dawn and climb up on them, watching nature around me. There are deer, kites, rabbits. I'm taken back to my childhood. My dad was a hunter and we spent many hours in the forest, simply observing nature. I feel a level of happiness and joy deep inside me that I haven't felt for a long time. After about a week, my body has adjusted to its new pace of life, the stillness around me slowly becomes a stillness within. It feels peaceful inside me. I could definitely get used to this.

CHAPTER 15
AWARENESS IS RISING

As I am becoming more aware of my thoughts, I am absolutely shocked and amazed by all the rubbish my mind produces pretty much non-stop all day. In one of our morning sessions, we talk about the fact that generally in our current society we have a tendency to focus on the negative. I think anyone who reads the paper or watches the news will agree. I had never thought about it until now. But made aware of it, it becomes so obvious. Remembering the negative was, of course, a really useful skill to have in our evolutionary development. To be able to tell your child, 'Don't eat that berry or that mushroom, because your great grandfather's best friend died from it, so we know it's poisonous,' is definitely a very useful ability humans have. It has protected us over many thousands of years and allowed us to survive.

However, we have become over-cautious. We now try to protect ourselves from all sorts of eventualities that most likely will never occur. There are dangers everywhere, be aware! This safety comes at a price, and the price many of us pay is our inner peace of mind. We are constantly alert, scanning our immediate surroundings for trouble, making sure we are prepared for whatever may come our way. Expect the worst! Like many people who develop cancers or other chronic illnesses, I am a worrier. According to the 3E Centre, you're more likely to get cancer if you have a tendency to worry. It's in my blood and I can now see that both my parents are worriers. No wonder I became one, too.

On one of my evening walks, I get an excellent example of this. I ring my dad. The setting sun is bathing the wheat field around me in the most delicious warm orange glow. We are chatting away and I tell him about my forest walks every morning and night, and how they remind me of our hunting days together and how they make me so happy.

And here it comes: the voice I have heard all my childhood, teenage-hood and adulthood. The voice of the concerned father who is also a worrier. "I really don't think you should be walking or jogging alone through a forest. Women get attacked, raped and murdered when they walk alone in remote areas. Who would hear you if you screamed?!" Immediately my whole body tenses up. Now I have my newly won awareness, I can literally watch my body change into fight-flight mode. Incredible. I pacify my dad, telling him that there are other people walking (which is a lie, I am often totally by myself) and that he needn't worry. We change the subject and eventually say our goodbyes. I take a deep breath.

Walking into the forest, I am replaying the conversation I just had over and over in my head. Doing this makes me tense again. When there is a little movement in some bushes to my left, I jump. My heart is pounding. My whole body is tuned into the imaginary dangers of the forest around me. I realise that my whole life I have actually always been a little 'on edge' when I walked by myself anywhere remote. This wouldn't matter too much for people who live in a city and don't walk anywhere. But I live in the countryside and walk my dog pretty much every day. For the first time ever, I notice how these walks, which could have been simply relaxing, were often accompanied by a slight undercurrent of fear or at least alertness. Tension instead of relaxation. I decide to become even more aware of how I feel, and to consciously change my emotion whenever I feel irrational fear. I'm really glad this happened. After all, I can only change things, if I bring them into my awareness. So much is happening subconsciously. Automatic reactions, automatic responses. Fear of possible dangers is definitely a pattern I see running through my whole family. I'm going to have to look at where that comes from.

Another emotion for me to watch is guilt. For years I have felt guilty about all sorts of things that I now realise are just rubbish.

> I felt guilty about having moved to the UK. I felt guilty about having left my family in Germany.
>
> I felt guilty about not being close when my parents both got cancer.
>
> I felt guilty about living so far from them that they couldn't see their grandson grow up the way they would have, had I stayed in Germany.
>
> I felt guilty about being a mum and working part-time instead of having a proper full blown career.
>
> I felt guilty about not being able to read Jack bedtime stories anymore, because I lost my voice.
>
> I felt guilty about being another ill wife for my husband.
>
> I felt guilty about not being happy with my life when to any outsider I had everything anyone could ever wish for.
>
> I felt guilty about feeling guilty.

On so many levels and seen from the outside, my life is a fairy-tale. I live in a lovely neighbourhood, our house is a dream home, exposed bricks in a rustic kitchen, an oak fireplace warming up the lounge; traditional features meet bright, vibrant fabrics in curtains and chairs. We have grown the most magical garden. My husband has his own successful business and we have no financial worries. He adores me, I adore him, and we love spending time together. I have a gorgeous son who is never any trouble. I am so blessed, yet feel so guilty as in my mind, I don't deserve any of it. My grandparents and parents taught me you have to work hard in order to get anything. I never feel I work hard enough, therefore I don't deserve what I have.

For years I have felt guilty about not being truly happy with my life. I wasn't exactly unhappy, but deep down and behind the functioning version of me, I felt something was missing. I was living my life somewhere parallel to where I should be. I had this image of two train tracks running parallel to each other and I was on the one track, when I should have been on the other: close, but not quite where I needed to be. Before my illnesses forced me to put my life on hold, I had no idea how to get from one track to the next. I needed a quantum leap. Something that seemed impossible in the Newtonian reality of my previous life and beliefs.

At school and at university, I was a top student. Learning came easily to me, because I loved it. Working part-time, translating and tutoring, there is definitely the feeling that 'I could have achieved so much more in my life', even though I have no idea yet what this more is. This lack of self-worth and self-esteem is another limiting belief I need to address. I love being a mum, and there is a part of me that really believes that there is no job more important in this world than to love and nurture the next generation of human beings and ensure the survival of our species. I'm not saying that all women should be mothers. On the contrary, all women should be able to choose to be whoever they wish to be. I have definitely devalued motherhood, however, and to find my inner peace, I am going to have to reframe how I see my role as a woman and mother.

I am not just becoming aware of all this hidden fear, worry and guilt, but also of how much I hid my true self in order to fulfil expectations I thought others had of me. Who am I? Who am I, when I am not just functioning for the world around me? Functioning is something many women, and especially the ones in my family, are incredibly good at. My own mum, my grandmother, my aunties all totally sacrificed their own dreams for the wellbeing of their family. I suddenly realise that my endometriosis started getting really bad about two years after I became a mum. Was this when I stopped looking after myself? I suppose like most first time mums, I copied the only true role model I had: my own mum.

At the Budwig Centre, with all this time on my hands, nowhere to rush to, and nothing to get distracted by, my perspective starts to shift. I am watching my own judgement of myself from an outsider's point of view and recognize how unnecessary my thoughts, fears, worries and all that guilt were. In the peace and quiet, I can finally see things with much more clarity. I can see that I have been an incredible mum. Deep down, I actually love caring, nurturing, cooking, baking and channelling lots of love into our home. I don't care two hoots about a successful career. Being a good mum is so much more important to me than earning a lot of money in some successful job.

Instead of feeling guilty for not being able to read Jack stories anymore, I can see that losing my voice has brought David and Jack closer. David took over as bedtime story reader and we have had the most beautiful family moments together, all cuddling up in bed at night. In truth, nobody missed out on anything, on the contrary, we have gained so much.

Instead of feeling guilty about being so far away from my parents, I can see that despite the geographical distance between the United Kingdom and Germany, my son has the most incredible relationship with his grandparents and we are all such a close, loving family. Maybe it is precisely the distance that makes us cherish our time together so much more. We don't waste it with squabbles, but actually value being together. Being ill myself also makes me realise that fighting an illness is a very personal journey. Even if I had lived closer when my parents were ill, they both would have still had to go on their own individual journey of healing.

Layer after layer I strip away beliefs I held onto for years. Day after day, I become aware of beliefs that are just not true. Who am I? What's left if I strip away everything that I believed I was? Will I be able to stop worrying? Will I be able to stop being afraid of things that most likely will never occur? Will I be able to switch off all that guilt? Can I really reinvent myself at the age of 40? What would the truest, most authentic version of me look like? Will the people I love still love me, if I drop all my facades and show the outside world who I truly am inside? Will turning myself inside out help me find whatever it is I have been missing in my life? Will all this letting go help me to heal myself?

CHAPTER 16
LISTENING TO MY NEEDS

Finding my true self is not an easy task, let me tell you. It is bloody hard to face all those stupid thoughts and beliefs that have been my reality for years. Admitting to myself that I might have been wrong is the hardest and equally the most liberating thing all at once. I'm sitting in the daily seminars, listening to how I need to be, in order to not stress anymore and all I can think is, 'They are describing my husband.' For years I have called him selfish. Could it be that he has been right and I have been wrong? My husband is someone who knows exactly who he is and what he wants. He doesn't do anything to simply please others. He says what he thinks, even if he knows others won't agree with him. He can spot people who are not authentic from a mile away and will avoid them if he can.

I am a people pleaser. I am very good at studying people, subconsciously knowing what makes them tick and being whoever they need me to be, so that they like me. I am the perfect chameleon. I do get on with pretty much everyone and find it incredibly easy to connect with people. But I morph into whatever the situation requires of me, rather than being my true self. I fill my life with things I don't actually want to do, just because I don't want to disappoint others. I go out of my way to help others, and often act against my own personal needs. It drives David crazy, when I put the wellbeing of others before my own, but in my belief system he is selfish and I am the good person.

Do I need to become more like David? Should I only offer help, when help is truly needed, instead of offering it even when I don't really have the time, strength and energy to do it? What do I really want to do? If I only consider myself and nobody else, what would I like my life to look like? The answers come easier than I expected. They've all been inside me for a while, I just didn't stop to listen. I need to stop teaching business German. I have loved it, but my voice really isn't good enough right now and I need to finally face the fact that I'm just not well enough. In addition, I always felt teaching languages wasn't what I truly came to this earth to do. Although officially my clients believe I will return to my lessons when I'm better (a friend has been covering my lessons), I have to admit to myself that I don't actually want to teach anymore. At least not languages.

I love Reiki. It gives me a buzz and my energy just soars when I treat others. Giving others a Reiki treatment, I feel like I am treating myself at the same time. I've already got my Reiki Level One and Two. Maybe I could work as a Reiki practitioner? I'd love to become a Reiki Master. That definitely goes on my 'to do list'. Reiki has reminded me how much I enjoy learning new things.

More personal development goes on my list. I'm not interested in earning money or having a career. I want to study what I'm passionate about, topics that interest me. My grandparents were refugees in the Second World War. They lost everything they owned and had to start from scratch. My grandmother always used to say to me, 'My girl, learn. What you've got in your head, nobody can take away from you.' I will learn again. I have always loved learning.

Last on my list is the thing that will be the hardest. The one thing that is the most important of all: to put myself first. To stop thinking about everyone else, before I think about myself. I am learning that I can only help others, if I am well. To be well, I need to look after myself. I know from past experience where 'not looking after myself' gets me. If I'm a rolled up bundle of pain, I'm no help to anyone. If I neglect myself, I cannot be the best mum, the best wife, the best friend, the best daughter or sister. I need to allow myself to rest and restore.

CHAPTER 17
GRATITUDE AND STILLNESS

I've always been taught to be grateful. Growing up in socialist East Germany, we didn't have much material wealth and I will always remember my dad teaching me to be happy with whatever it is I've got. I definitely learned to find happiness in the small things: a flower, birdsong, a ray of sunshine, being together with my loved ones. All this was a massive part of my upbringing, but I realize here at the Centre, how much the unification of Germany, the fall of socialism and subsequent exposure to capitalism had thrown me out of my own inner balance.

The Berlin Wall came down just before my thirteenth birthday. Suddenly, I was a teenager trying to survive in a world that my parents were more lost in than us kids. I observed and tried to learn from television, newspapers, magazines and West Germans I met, what this new world expected of me. I felt at odds with many of the capitalist values. Everyone seemed to be looking out for themselves first. I so desperately tried to fit in, but this new system was totally out of alignment with the values I had grown up with. It seemed to me, that capitalism was all about individuality, about trusting nobody but yourself, when I had come from a society of community and being stronger together. Even now, my childhood values were in total confrontation with the British middle class life I was living. Most people seemed to never be happy with what they had, everyone seemed to be in a race for bigger, faster, more. Whenever I tried to be like that, I felt at odds with myself. Whenever I was me, I felt at odds with the world.

With time on my hands to reflect, I realise how in those years of transitioning from Eastern to Western values, I started losing sight of who I truly was. To fit in, I made sure that - like everyone else - I was busy. Running from A to B, filling every minute of the day with some sort of activity. The trouble is: if you are busy, you cannot listen to your true self. In order to hear that inner voice, you need to be still. I had rediscovered this stillness when I first learned Reiki. Here at the 3E Centre in Germany, I am now consciously practicing this stillness all day long, and I am becoming aware of its effects on my whole being. It's a game changer.

Besides daily meditations, we are asked to write a gratitude journal. Every night we have to write down five things that happened each day that we are grateful for, things that brought us joy: our 'five stars of the day'. The first few days it is quite hard to write this list. Knowing I need five things for my list each night, I start making mental notes during the day of all the things that put a smile on my face. Slowly, my awareness shifts from pain and 'everything I haven't got' to 'all the things I have got'. Looking at my daily five star diary entries, the things that bring me joy are incredibly simple.

> Watching nature.
> Doing everything more slowly.
> Reading.
> Drawing.
> Learning something new.
> Listening to birdsong.
> Speaking to my family.
> Interesting chats within our group.
> Finding stillness.
> The reflection of a ray of sunshine on the trees.
> Watching butterflies.
> A forest walk.
> Starting my day with yoga in the garden.
> Eating cherries off a tree.

Watching the sunset.
Smiling at a stranger.

Reading this list, I realise that none of it requires money. It's all there, right in front of me. And it's free. All I have to do is open my eyes, become aware and take time out from the distractions of the busy world around me. Why do we focus so much on earnings and material wealth, when what actually makes us happy cannot be bought? The truly life-changing realisations can be very simple indeed.

CHAPTER 18
LAUGHTER AND HAPPINESS

I'm changing. I cannot wipe the smile off my face. Everywhere I look, there is life to be noticed. I sit on a log watching ants. I imagine being them, carrying leaves a hundred times the size of my own body. I pretend to fly with the butterflies from flower to flower, a playful expression of life, caressed by the warmth of a ray of sunshine. I sway with the yellow summer wheat dancing in the wind. The blue corn flowers smile back at me, reflecting the blue sky overhead. The wild cherries growing on the edge of a field are the sweetest, juiciest cherries I have ever tasted! The world is so beautiful!

I am being brainwashed. And I like it. 'I am ill and I hate my endometriosis' becomes, 'A small part of me is currently not well, but the vast majority of my body's cells work absolutely fine and I'm grateful for that.' The cul-de-sac of pain I had lived in for so many years becomes a vast ocean of possibilities for improvement. If you hit rock bottom, things can only get better. I am starting to feel so much better!

One of our favourite classes takes place every Wednesday afternoon and it is called laughing yoga. We all stand in a circle, our outstretched arms become the wings of an eagle. Our circle of healing bodies is flying high above the clouds, becoming one in the psychedelic music that fills the room. We follow the instructions of our teacher. The eagle lands and turns into a monkey. OO-AA, curled up monkey arms as we jump around, letting go of all inhibitions. To start with, we self-consciously watch each other. After a few minutes, we just let rip. All inhibitions are gone. We are laughing our heads off. If you walked into the room you would most likely wonder if you accidentally entered a lunatic asylum.

I am learning, that my brain cannot distinguish between a fake and a real smile. Just moving the edges of the mouth upwards into a smile triggers the brain to release endorphins into the blood stream. Endorphins are also called happiness hormones. Laughing yoga is based on this automatic happiness response. You just laugh: little shy laughs, fully blown belly laughs - hahaha, huhuhu, hihihi. While I start off just pretending to laugh, which morphs into laughing at my own silliness, my laughs soon become genuine until the whole group laughs so much we can't stop. I feel like I have taken happiness drugs. There is a lightness inside that makes me feel free. Free to just be. It is addictive. I want to feel like that all the time.

Is it really this easy to be happy? Can I fake it till I make it? Practicing happiness through all these mental exercises we do - positive affirmations, positive rephrasing of everything we say, meditations, visualisations, laughing yoga - seems to actually result in us all becoming happier.

Try it while you read this. Smile and see how it changes how you feel.

CHAPTER 19
THE LANGUAGE OF OUR BODY

What if illnesses are the way our body lets us know that we are doing something that is not good for us? At the Centre they believe each illness is a message from the body. They specialise in cancer and claim that the cancer you get is linked to the type of person you are, the experiences you've gone through and the beliefs or worries you carry within you. The in-house cancer specialist explains that she can often tell after a few minutes what sort of cancer a person has. Apparently, there are very typical patterns for the different types of cancer. I find this fascinating. If illnesses are a specific message from our body, do we just have to learn to decode the messages? Cancer and most chronic illnesses like endometriosis are linked to stress and stress is primarily caused by our thoughts. It is not what happens around us that stresses us, it's what we make it mean. What meaning we give to an event is based on our own individual experience: if ten people in a room all experienced the same thing, you would get ten different stories of what happened, as each person would interpret the events based on their belief system.

As the 3E Centre specialises in cancer, and not endometriosis, they cannot tell me what the endometriosis pattern might be. When I start looking into the typical cancer patterns, a light bulb is switched on and I can so clearly recognise my own family members aligning with the patterns of their own cancer.

> Bowel cancer (my dad) is linked to self-esteem issues.

> Thyroid cancer (my mum) - issues around speaking your mind or suppressing what you want to say.
>
> Lung cancer is linked to grief (my paternal grandfather died 6 months after my grandmother, he grieved her death and didn't want to live without her).
>
> Cervical cancer (my maternal grandmother) - issues around womanhood, femininity and creating the life you want to live.
>
> Breast cancer - issues around nurturing and over nurturing, often over nurturing others and under nurturing oneself.
>
> Brain tumours (my aunt) – issues around control, trying to control your life too much or feeling out of control in your life.
>
> Liver cancer – the liver holds anger, so people who get very angry tend to develop liver cancer.

On the one hand, it sounds totally crazy that the beliefs of a person are linked to the type of cancer they get. On the other hand, the patterns for each cancer certainly seem to fit the cancer sufferers I know. Or am I just making them fit? Am I reading into it what I want to see? In any case, I decide I will have to look into this further. There seems to be a recurring pattern connecting the women in my family. My maternal grandmother died of cervical cancer, my mother had a hysterectomy for what we now believe may also have been endometriosis. I have endometriosis. What is the pattern linking us all? Our illnesses all affect the female reproductive system. Is that what I need to explore? What is the message of endometriosis? What is laryngeal papillomatosis and losing my voice trying to tell me? Can the life coach and therapist here help me find out what limiting belief patterns subconsciously run inside me, causing my illnesses and preventing me from healing? What is my body trying to tell me? What do I need to hear?

There is something else that according to the centre plays a role in chronic illnesses. These illnesses have become chronic because the body, for some reason, either cannot or does not want to heal them. Why would I not want to heal? Surely nobody wants to be ill? I am learning that specifically in chronic conditions, the body can perceive the illness as something beneficial, something worth holding onto. A benefit that arises from being ill is called a secondary gain. A secondary gain refers to some advantage that your illness is giving you. We subconsciously hold onto the illness, because it provides something we wanted, but didn't get before we became ill. This is obviously not a conscious process, nobody would consciously choose to be ill or in pain. There are many different reasons, why we might hold onto the state of being ill.

Here are just a few examples to illustrate the point. When you're ill, suddenly people care for you, you are being looked after, you get a level of attention you might have longed for, but never got. If you get healthy again, all the love and attention you receive while ill may disappear again, leaving you as lonely and abandoned as you felt before becoming ill. This might be a reason to subconsciously not want to return back to being healthy. Financial security is another example for not wanting to become healthy. Becoming ill may have allowed you to leave a job you didn't like. If you became healthy again, you may have to return to this job, lose financial benefits or a disability status the illness has provided you with. The illness gives you a reason to exist. Without it, there would not be much to do. This is often a reason for older people or people who have lost their purpose in life. Suddenly there are appointments in their calendar: doctors, specialists. Your disease becomes your job, so to speak. As bizarre as this sounds, but recovering from it would mean going back to a life without purpose. So people subconsciously hold onto the illness instead. Being ill is a great excuse to get out of doing things you do not want to do. It allows you to say no. No to seeing certain people, no to attending events.

Holding onto the illness and not wanting to let it go over a long period of time turns the disease into a chronic condition. This is interesting. I am reflecting on this for my two illnesses. What am I gaining? Why would I subconsciously hold on to them and prevent myself from healing? What is my body saying to me?

It looks like I need to learn a new language again. I have studied German, English, French and Russian. This time, however, I'm not learning a language to communicate with the outside world, I'm learning it to communicate with my inside world. Just like it takes time to learn a normal language, it will take time to learn the language of my body. I realise that this won't happen overnight; it's a process. To unravel thirty nine years of conditioning might take longer than the four weeks I've got in Germany.

Healing naturally is a bit like removing layers of an onion. When you've removed one layer, the next one appears, but you cannot deal with the next layer, unless you remove the one before that. My own next layer of healing reveals itself when I have my weekly appointment with the Centre's doctor. We look at my voice and he says I can't speak because there is an emotional blockage somewhere that needs to be removed.

"I recommend you try kinesiology in order to find the root cause for your endometriosis and the lost voice," he suggests. I hadn't really come across kinesiology before arriving here, but by coincidence or fate one of my fellow co-patients is a qualified kinesiologist, which means I can start my discovery journey right here, right now. Sitting in the garden, on a beautiful summer's afternoon, we do what in kinesiology is called a muscle test.

It is one of the most fascinating things I have ever witnessed. Kinesiology also believes my body knows what it needs better than my mind does. I can ask it simple questions, and it will answer with yes, no or maybe. To ensure it is my body and not my mind answering, I have to hold my arm stretched out in front of me and the kinesiologist is pushing down on it. My arm answers yes by staying strong and firm, maybe by wavering, and no by collapsing. I'm a little doubtful at first, but am utterly amazed when my arm takes on a life of its own, going into an independent yes-no-maybe conversation with my kinesiologist friend.

The end result points to my female family ancestry line, in particular my maternal grandmother and my mother. My body tells me that subconsciously I don't trust life, because I believe life causes pain and suffering. Having linked life with pain and suffering, I'm scared to live life fully, because I'm afraid the pain and suffering will increase along with the life force I allow myself to embody. Instead of living the life I'd like to live, I keep my life force down. Suffering the way I do, subconsciously validates this core belief I have created: life is hard, life means suffering, life is painful.

According to Dr. Bruce Lipton, who wrote a whole book about the biology of belief[11], core beliefs are often created in the first six years of our lives, when we watch the people around us and subconsciously copy their beliefs. I can see how both my grandmother and mother held the belief that life was hard, especially for women. The message I received as a child from the women in my family was that men have a much better life. Society tells us we are the weaker sex, however much every woman intuitively knows that this is not true. The days of the warrior goddesses of old have long gone, the womb of a mother is no longer seen as sacred for holding the seed of life. Being a woman in my family is not seen as something desirable. I can see how my

---

[11] Dr. Bruce Lipton: The Biology of Belief. Hay House, 2015.

failing belief in the power of womanhood might be linked to my failing reproductive organs. My sense of femininity is definitely out of balance. I have always rejected being a woman. Is this why I developed an illness like endometriosis, an illness that effects the very area in the body where my female power resides.

For my voice, writing comes up. I want to write, but I'm scared to show the world who I truly am, I'm also scared of being judged, I'm scared of not being good enough. Again, the female aspect comes in, this time as the female voice that feels suppressed and in a way probably has been suppressed in Western society for thousands of years. I've got an English literature degree and as a young student loved the works of George Elliot, Jane Austen and the Bronte sisters. In the nineteenth century, many female writers had to hide their identities as women and could only get published by pretending to be men. Could I be a writer, like them? My grandmother always used to say she should write a book about her life. I feel that whatever blockage there is, it's something I need to heal for both of us. Is it my job to write her story? My story? Will writing it all down help release the blockage in my throat, the growths that are actually stopping me from speaking right now? I have some handwritten pages my grandmother wrote, before she died of cervical cancer. I think to truly understand myself, I have to understand her suffering.

CHAPTER 20
MY GRANDMOTHER'S STORY

I feel I owe it to my grandmother to actually include the original words she has written, which I translated from German to English. For better understanding I have minimally changed some sentences, indicated in *[square brackets]*. I am leaving the rest exactly as she wrote it in a little notebook during the last weeks of her life. The original switches between present and past tenses, which I left in the translation. She had often said to me, that her life would be worthy of a book. So here is her book, within my book.

> *My dearest,*
>
> *I was born on 7 May 1921 in [a village in the Sudetenland, an area in the Czech Republic on the border to Germany]. My dad was a cattle merchant, my mum a florist. In 1924, dad died of a heart attack. Mum ran the shop and she had some female home workers binding dried flower arrangements for her. Mother died in 1930. She was in [the nearest town] for an operation and got a lung infection. I can still hear grandfather's cries: his favourite daughter was dead and he now had to keep his promise and look after me and my sister. In 1931, he fell ill and returned to his own apartment. His eldest daughter cared for him until he died of bowel cancer.*
>
> *Now, things went downhill. My half-sister did her own thing and didn't much care about me. In*

1932, I was sent to an orphanage. There was little to eat, meat was never to be seen. We had to get up at 6am, go to church at 7am and afterwards to school. My legal guardian must have paid the fees regularly, but otherwise nobody looked out for me. Once a month there was a visiting day. Nobody ever came for me.

On 1 July 1935, aged 14, my guardian took me to work as a maid in a household. It was like a prison. Mountains of laundry and all had to be washed by hand. My bed was under the roof, on winter mornings there was snow on it!

In 1937, I found a better job. I had some people I knew from school and sometimes visited their relatives. I had to work hard, but you can endure everything, when you don't know any different. For the first time, I had a chance to socialise a bit more: once a fortnight, I had Sunday afternoon off. In 1938, I met your [grand]father. My legal guardian went berserk, he laid into me. For years nobody in the wider family had cared about me, but now all hell broke loose. October 1938 fighting broke out, people talked about war. The Germans fled to Saxony and the Czechs smashed everything to pieces.

I lived alone in the villa. Finally, the soldiers left and Hitler 'liberated' the Sudentenland – what a 'nice' liberation it was. I earned 18.50 Mark monthly salary.

Peace was short-lived. On 3 June 1939, I got married. It was a tiny ceremony in a small chapel. At least I now had a roof over my head. Granddad still had work and I had sold 2.5 hectares of agricultural land, which enabled us to buy some furniture. The money that my parents had left me had been spent by my legal guardian. Stupid as we were, we just accepted it and never did a thing about it. I still had my parents' house. The house was mine, but I had five tenants who all paid a meagre 15 Marks rent. I could have done with someone in my life with a bit of drive or dexterity.

First of September 1939 – war with Poland. The people are becoming uneasy. Hitler the criminal leads us into disaster. The men are being conscripted and the first ones die in Poland. On 2 January 1940, grandpa has to leave. There are ration cards and I somehow get by doing some home based work: weaving belts and sewing trousers.

Twice a week I walk to [the neighbouring village] to visit auntie Mieli. Uncle Joseph has also moved in. I help them work the fields and I make the butter. I always get some food there and can take a piece of butter and some eggs with me. That way, my life isn't too bad.

On 26 April 1940, our son Peter was born. Grandpa was in France. All the young girls have to work in ammunition factories. The numbers are dwindling, every day Germans die in foreign lands. I get 68 Mark support, 15 Marks go for rent, which leaves me with 50 Marks a month to survive on. Everything is possible if needs must.

In August, Peter gets ill with whooping cough. I do not have a single quiet minute anymore and I am always alone. There is no remedy against whooping cough. He gets weaker by the day, all I can do is feed him breastmilk from a tiny teaspoon. When he coughs, it all comes out again. The doctor says: 'Let the poor child die in peace. A baby cannot survive this illness.' Day and night I try to feed him, he is all

I have. I'm down to 48 kilos. After four long months, the cough finally subsides and he slowly improves, by spring we're through the worst of it.

Grandpa is in Greece, his last leave was upsetting, the Germans are not doing well. But the madness continues. Grandpa gets posted to Africa. I get by somehow. Post is rare, if you want to get any information at all, you have to tune into a foreign radio station. It's forbidden, but every now and again we risk it and try. In 1943, granddad is captured in Tunesia. After 6 months, I receive a postcard from the Red Cross. From now on I receive a card every now and then from a prisoner of war camp in Texas.

On 7 May 1945 the Russians arrive. They storm into the houses and take everything they need. We live in constant fear. By the middle of May the first Czechs arrive together with some partisan fighters. The Germans are being robbed and many are shot dead. Everyone has their own way of finding revenge.

In June 1945, my parents-in-law are being picked up. At 5am in the morning, the Red Army and two Czech soldiers knock on the door and shout, 'Out!' We quickly pack a few things into a hand cart, the Czechs take our keys. They leave me behind with my little boy, alone in the house. The old couple scream and shout as they are leaving, but the Russians just laugh at them. Four weeks later, people are shot daily in the streets of our little town, the teachers are beaten and imprisoned. Fear is growing.

On 10 July 1945 the big deportation begins. All Germans have to leave town. At 5am in the morning, we start off, 500 of us are being horded together in the market place. Then we have to march 5km to the nearest border crossing to Germany. The Czechs rob us of everything we carry. I no longer own a thing: I'm left with the pushchair, one pillow and 200 Marks I had hidden under my shirt that they miraculously did not find. Peter has a temperature of 40.

In Saxony, the communists greet us shouting 'Nazis' at us, the Russians are hunting us down, nobody is allowed out on the streets after 8pm. An old woman kindly takes me in. I try one last time to get over the border, desperate to pick up just a few things from our old house. I tie my little boy onto my back, but on the way back they catch me and everything I had picked up is taken off me. Wherever I go, bad luck seems to follow me. I can no longer stay near the border and we have no more food.

Peter lives off once slice of bread a day, which the children are given. They have to go themselves to pick it up. I leave with the aim to get to the countryside. Where there are farms, there is food. I get to Wurzen, but the bridge has been destroyed. It takes me a week to get from Dresden to Magdeburg. We travel in cattle trucks. Again and again we're being disconnected, because the Russians need the train. [I remember my grandmother telling me that they were locked into the cattle trucks like animals. Some babies died and just got thrown out of the train, so the dead bodies would not cause disease.]

Once in Magdeburg, I didn't know where to go. The Americans were retreating, the Russians took over the region. After many hours, there was a train to a town near the village where Berta lived. I decided to go get on it, as I knew Berta's parents had a small farm. [My grandfather and Berta's husband did their army training together and the women had once met when the men were on leave. Berta would become my grandmother's best friend.]

In the village, the surprise was big. Nobody had any idea that the Germans had been thrown out of the Sudetenland. There was no radio and no newspaper. A local family took me in and we at least had some food. I helped in the fields and that's how we got by from 1945 till 1946 without any money.

The only thing I knew about grandpa was that he was a prisoner of war in Texas. I hadn't received any post for over a year. The village was now occupied by the Russians. Every night, people fled through the river into the West. When some refugees passed through, I gave them a postcard addressed to the prisoner of war camp. Miraculously, the postcard actually arrived and granddad now at least knew where I was.

On 16 July 1946, grandpa arrived. He had come through the river at night. Peter was six years old. He had never met his dad and only ever called him uncle. He never got used to having a father. In October 1948 we got two rooms at the vicarage, but there was no wood and no coal. I could write a novel, nobody would believe how we lived. We somehow made ends meet, working for the local farmers. In 1947, grandpa gets a job in construction, earning 84 pennies an hour. We chop wood in the winter, I knit a little and swap some of my knitting for the odd tin of sausage meat. We feed a few rabbits and our little Peter has to get food for them. It's a sad childhood for him. This has always saddened me deeply. In 1948, our first daughter [my mum] is born. We have to move again, this time into two damp and cold attic rooms. A human being can endure a lot!

In January 1949 our boy falls ill: he has a temperature on Sunday, by Wednesday he is dead. There was no medicine, they simply said 'meningitis' and that was it. With difficulties we finally managed to find a carpenter to make us a coffin. All I wanted to do was die. But always in the darkest hours, help came from somewhere. I don't know how I survived all this.

In 1950, our second daughter was born, another little bundle of sorrow. Grandpa finds work in a nearby town. Houses are being built and he earns enough so we can eat. In 1952, I find agricultural work and earn a few Marks. The little one goes to nursery, a small suitcase full of spare pants in hand. Her older sister has to look after her when I go to work in the afternoons from 1-6pm.

In 1957, the big agricultural reform happens and the agricultural cooperative is formed. That wasn't easy. The farmers land is confiscated and they all leave to go to the West. The land lies in ruin.

In 1959 we move from the village to the town. I still work at the plant nursery in the village from 1960-62. On 2 June 1962, I find work as a cook in the army canteen. I earned 280 Marks. In 1964, I qualify as a proper chef and earn 380 Marks. The girls, thank God, are doing well at school and with diligence and hard work they both manage to learn the professions they wanted. I always worried. I suppose that's normal for a mum who didn't experience much good in her life. Granddad only ever worked and kept the money together. We *wanted the children to have a better life than we did. Did we succeed? Often, they didn't understand us. Our life had been so hard and every time we thought it got better, the next disaster would happen.*

In 1992, my illness starts. I have no idea how I got through it all. My desperation at times is beyond words. I often think, this is the end, but a human being can and must endure a lot. 24 July 1992: hospital. Diagnosis: Cervical cancer. Total hysterectomy and 5 rounds of radiation therapy.

1993: a bad smear test, hospital again. Vaginal cancer. November and December: chemotherapy. On 17 December 1993 I lose all my hair and have to get a wig. I'm close to a nervous breakdown. I cannot count the tears I've cried. They tell me to recover throughout January, so they can operate in February.

In March 1994, my third chemo starts. I'm going downhill, my bloods are awful, I am constantly tired and can hardly breathe. Despite my bad bloods, they are doing another chemo. Eventually, I get blood transfusions. I recover a little, only to be given another chemo in May. On 15 May is my granddaughter's confirmation. We have visitors to stay and all I want is peace and quiet. I'm exhausted, cannot do a single thing. Another blood transfusion follows. The last chemo is cancelled, I'm too weak. End of June, a check up shows that the chemos did not work.

In July 1994, another operation follows, I was in horrendous pain: every day they wash the wound with saline solution and hydrogen, it is barbaric! I come out of hospital in July. The next check-up in November shows no abnormalities, but its early days yet. In January 1995 I have another check-up. My days are probably numbered. An MRI scan shows more cancer cells, more radiation therapy is suggested. I am in unbearable pain. I get 23 radiation sessions in June and July. Do they really think this will help? The bladder gets radiation damage, I have metastases in the lung. What is the point? The pain is indescribable, the bladder treatments are agony. Now I am having difficulties breathing and I start coughing. I long for peace.

On a daily basis, things get worse. Now the bladder stops working completely. I am so tired. I can't go on any more. If you ever experience hard times in your life, read these lines and think about how I suffered. Were I a dog or a cat, they would have put me down long ago, but as a human you're worth nothing.

In November 1995 I am in hospital again with kidney problems. They say only an operation can help: the bladder needs to be taken out. 20 November is the operation, I'm in a bad way. No air, no strength. 2 December 1995, I can finally go home. I can hardly walk. Anna has to change the catheter bags, I cannot go on, I have no strength left. Now my bowel starts troubling me. Only God knows what comes next. I hope it won't be long anymore.

1996: the bowel is the most painful. I had the flu which totally flattened me, coughing still hurts.

These were the last lines she wrote. In July 1995, I left Germany to be an Au pair in England. Returning home for the Christmas holiday, both my grandmother and I intuitively knew that this was the last time we would see each other, the last time we would hug, our last goodbye. We both cried our eyes out, trying to stay strong but failing miserably. Neither of us could actually speak the words out loud, nor say what we both knew. We just hugged and didn't want to let go of the other. A croaky, suffocating 'Good bye' all we could muster. I will forever be grateful for that final goodbye in December 1995. My grandmother passed away in May 1996.

My grandmother's experience confirmed my core belief that life is pain and suffering. Her story is the foundation for so much of my own journey, a journey that turned my reality into daily endometriosis pain and suffering. I am only just beginning to understand how much she has influenced me (we were extremely close) and how much of her suffering I have subconsciously carried on my own shoulders (or in my womb). The pointless pain she had to endure while following medical cancer protocol may well have influenced me all these years later to search for alternative options to mainstream endometriosis treatments. Maybe this is where my deep inner knowing and my often stubborn insistence that 'there must be another way' originated. Watching her hope for healing so brutally crushed by the side effects of the cancer treatments she received, watching her fade away slowly and in unimaginable pain for the sake of prolonging her life by a few more months, I slowly learned that there is a difference between living and existing. In hindsight, the months she got were not worth the price she had to pay for them. Witnessing her ordeal gave me the courage all these years later to keep searching, even when there was seemingly no point in doing so. To this day, her strength is what I connect to when I feel I can no longer go on. Her courage inspires me to never give up. Whatever problems I might face, they seem nothing compared to the hardships she endured. And despite all of it, she was still able to give so much love. Thank you, grandma', for having been part of my life. I will forever carry you in my heart.

CHAPTER 21

PASSED ON TRAUMA - HEALING MY ANCESTRY LINE

My grandmother was a strong, emancipated, independent woman who gave me so much love. We were incredibly close. I would spend every holiday with her. She cherished being able to spend quality time with her granddaughters, time she hadn't been able to give to her own daughters during the difficult post war years. As a child, I could never understand the sadness in her eyes. Reading her story, it's no wonder it was there. I think through us granddaughters, she finally got to witness the happy, carefree childhood every child should be able to live.

There was another thing that, as a child, I would not have been able to put into words: a certain negative energy my grandmother had around men. To her, all men were a disappointment, men were not to be relied upon, men were a nuisance, men were trouble. The incredible strength she incorporated as a woman was juxtaposed by her total disdain towards 'the male'. My grandfather seemed to silently accept that side of her, sitting in his armchair whistling, retreating into a world in his head that only he had access to. Maybe he still remembered a different, pre-war version of his wife and that enabled him not to judge. All her love seemed to be reserved for me and my cousin, her little girls. She doted on us and could literally not spoil us enough. I was a picky eater, so she would go to the butcher and buy the most expensive pork fillet to make my favourite meal, Schnitzel. Lovingly, she would beat up the egg whites from her own chickens to make lemon mousse, my favourite dessert. My cousin would get boiled potatoes with butter and salt every time she asked, even for breakfast. Patiently she would sit with us girls, teaching us how to knit our own jumpers, crochet coasters and place mats, praising us along the way, lovingly correcting our mistakes, encouraging us every step of the way. My own mum was often busy being a mum. My grandmother knew what I liked and what I needed. She was the stillness and creative silence I craved.

After her death, her best friend told us a part of my grandmother's story that she had been too ashamed to include in her handwritten notebook. Something nobody ever mentioned and something that her daughters never knew. A hidden piece of her life story, that explains so much of her behaviour. As a young woman working in the fields after the war, my grandmother was gang raped by a whole group of drunk Russian soldiers. The rape left her with such horrendous wounds that she had to be taken to hospital, her whole vaginal area shredded to pieces by the violent intrusion into the most private and sacred parts of her womanhood. Her femininity needed to be stitched back together, leaving scars behind that never truly healed in her lifetime.

It was the missing puzzle piece without which the picture we had of her never quite made sense. Here was the perfectly understandable reason why she disliked men, and absolutely abhorred drunken men. My mum remembers her mother consumed by worry, when her daughters had become teenagers and young women, especially at weekends when they were out dancing with friends. Back then, my mum and her sister didn't understand why their mother would be out on her bike at night searching the town for her daughters, if they were a few minutes late, if they'd danced a bit longer and hadn't returned home exactly at the agreed time. They didn't understand why their mother was always so worried about them, why she couldn't be more relaxed like other mothers were.

My own mother grew up with an incredible, inexplicable fear of drunken men. Such overpowering, all consuming fear that she had no rational explanation for, yet equally couldn't free herself from. Nothing had ever happened to my mum involving drunk men, but she hated being around them and was scared stiff by them. Subconsciously, she had taken on her own mother's fear of drunk men, a fear totally justified after what had happened to her. My mum, unaware of this subconscious pattern, became a slave to that fear. This in turn created lots of conflict between my mother and father. My dad came from a family of pub owners and had grown up in an environment where alcohol was a normal ingredient to collective joy and merriment. My dad was always a happy drunk: he would sing, laugh and be jolly. Because my mum had internalised her own mother's energy of fear around drunk men, she would be scared by my dad when he returned home after a party. He could never understand this, and felt offended that she could think he would hurt her. All he wanted was to be loved, cuddled and accepted for who he was, yet she was trapped in her own fear, unable to go anywhere near him. Argument after argument ensued for years, both of them repeating their subconscious patterns. I remember being in the middle of their arguments, trying to mediate their unreasonable behaviour. I didn't understand my mum's reaction. I could feel her fear, but could not see any justification for it. For my mum, finally knowing her own mother's rape story and understanding where her own fear came from, eventually allowed her to free herself from it.

Slowly, I'm starting to see all the interconnections, how all of us are part of an intricate web of patterns and beliefs. For many years, I have carried the knowledge of my grandmother's suffering with me. Many times I have cried for her, for everything she went through, everything she endured, so that eventually, I could have one of the best grandmothers in the world. By emotionally going through her pain, however, I've been suffering myself. All this is coming up during my therapy sessions at the Centre. I have never really dealt with it all: the loss, the pain. My own mother had a hysterectomy at 42. Have we all carried this trauma in us energetically? Can I now heal it for all of us, so it at least doesn't get passed on to the next generation?

I write. I cry. I write. I cry. Slowly, the suppressed emotions I had buried for years are leaving my body. I can physically feel the muscles in my lower tummy area relaxing and I am releasing tensions that have been there since I started menstruating. The Indian Chakra system teaches us that the sacral chakra, the area below the naval where our sexual organs reside, is our pleasure centre. Chakras are energy centres in our body, according to ancient Indian teachings, we have seven main chakras, each one linked to certain organs and certain emotions. When our emotions are thrown out of balance, these energy centres become unbalanced, and the belief is that this will eventually lead to physical illnesses in the organs corresponding to the chakras. The sacral chakra is balanced when we enjoy life, when we create the life we truly want to live. This chakra, or energy centre, is linked to our reproductive system, which is where physical life is created: the baby growing inside a woman's womb. Do my unbalanced beliefs around what it means to be a woman find their physical expression in endometriosis? It is my rejection of womanhood and my perceived powerlessness as a woman to create the life I want (as supposed to the life others want for me) that have resulted in endometriosis? Is it a coincidence that endometriosis is an illness that causes infertility and actually makes me physically unable to produce life?

I start working through my own limiting beliefs of womanhood and motherhood. Suddenly, I see with such clarity, that the painful periods I have always had, started to turn into unbearable endometriosis pain after I became a mother myself. I see the pattern: my grandmother, my own mother, now me as a mother. I see how all of us stopped creating the life we dreamed of, when we became mothers. I see the sacrifice that mothers make for their children, passed down from one generation to the next. I see how all three of us turned life into duty, filled with chores from morning to night, instead of seeing it as the wondrous, joyful experience it should be. As I am working through all this, I also remember weird dreams and visions I had as a child that I never understood: needle like pains in my vagina from as young as five, six years old that would occur in dreams. Pains that I knew were connected to men, long before I had any awareness of sexual intercourse. I remember dreams as a teenager and young woman, in which a row of men would queue to have sex with me. Is it possible that experiences of one's ancestors are projected into one's own energy field subconsciously? Can trauma be passed on from one generation to the next through our shared energy fields?

In a powerful meditation, my life coach gives me the chance to heal my ancestry line. I'm lying on a mattress on the floor of one of the therapy rooms, covered by a blanket. I'm all warm and cosy, while my coach's voice takes me on a beautiful walk down a mountain path, into a peaceful meadow, through a ravine and into an open valley surrounded by high cliffs. I'm kneeling on the floor, my mum and dad appear before me. They smile, blessing me with their parental love. Then they step behind me, facing the same way I'm facing. I'm still kneeling. My mum is standing to my left, her right hand protectively and lovingly resting on my left shoulder. My dad is standing to my right, with his left hand on my right shoulder. Their parents take their place behind them. My mum's parents behind her, my dad's parents behind him. There are now 4 people standing behind my mum and dad, then eight parents take their place behind my grandparents and so on and so forth. Each mother on the left, each father on the right, standing protectively behind their child, hands resting on their offspring's shoulders. Generation after generation of parents and children, all connected. Like a big funnel my ancestors are all behind me, hands on shoulders, parents sending love down the ancestry line via their children to the next generation.

FROM ENDO WAR TO INNER PEACE

I know, that what we call reality is me lying there, on a mattress, covered by a blanket. I know, that this is what the world of reason would make me believe is the whole of reality. No more. But my experience is so much more than that. In fact, the reality of my physical body totally disappears. I am in the valley. I can feel my parents and all my ancestors. I can feel their love. It feels so powerful, so real, even though I know it's only in my mind. I don't care that this makes no rational sense. I know that judging from most normal people's perspective, including my own before I arrived here at the Centre, all this might sound utterly crazy. My coach asks me to imagine she is my grandmother. What would I say to her? What words remained unspoken? If I could stand opposite her right now, what would I do? My eyes well up. I hug her. All I want to say, all I need her to know so desperately, all that comes out of my mouth is 'I love you so much.' The whole exercise is so simple, yet it changes something profound in me. I feel free. I don't know what happened or how it works, but I know that whatever I am experiencing here at the Centre is working its magic. I am starting to feel better, lighter and more positive.

When I go to the toilet that day, there are grey pieces of dead skin tissue in my stool. I am scared when I first see this, but a sense of hope mingles with the initial fear. After all, I have just learned in one of our lectures that the body detoxes through the bowel, bladder and skin. Emotionally I am letting go of a lot of negativity and tension. Is the detoxification, the healthy nutrition and the emotional release allowing my body to let go of the dis-ease on a physical level? I imagine the grey lifeless bits in my toilet are dead endometriosis tissue. I decide to trust my gut and to take what is happening as a good sign, rather than as something to worry about. After all, it is not what happens to me, but what I make it mean, that governs whether my life is positive or negative. I have a choice: I can chose trust over worry and fear.

Having worked through my grandmother's story, looking at the links to my mother's behaviour and belief patterns, and in turn my own patterns is bringing a sense of deep clarity into my perception. I've been sitting in front of lots of puzzle pieces and suddenly I am starting to see how they fit together. I can see where certain patterns or false beliefs originated. I can see how they served as a form of protection, but were actually limiting me.

My grandmother - due to her own experience of having to fend for herself for years - always drummed it into me that I should never ever rely on a man or husband to look after me. She always said, I needed to learn, study and make sure I earn my own money, so I can provide for myself. When I became a mother, I insisted on going back to work part time the minute my statutory maternity allowance stopped after six months. I put myself under constant pressure as I had to fulfil my grandmother's requirement of being able to provide for myself and my child, should the need arise. I totally stressed over money, when there was absolutely no need. I was in the lucky position that whatever I earned was my own pocket money and it wasn't really needed to pay household bills. In my mind, however, I always felt I wasn't working hard enough, I wasn't good enough, I could do better, push myself more. All this stress I created myself, totally unnecessarily and I can suddenly see this so clearly.

My life coach recommends a book called, *The forgotten generation. The war children break their silence*[2]. It's a German book about the whole generation of children born during or shortly after the Second World War to parents that had been deeply traumatised. Parents who were often emotionally shut off. In a way, I can understand how they had to cut themselves off from their emotions, in order to survive everything they had lived through. My grandparents were parents, whose main goal was to ensure there was enough food on the table and the kids had a roof over their head. Parents, who had no concept of their children's emotional needs beyond those of pure survival. Reading the book, I can see my own parents, my aunts, my uncles. The book calls them the forgotten generation that had to function, that grew up in a life devoid of emotions. I am seeing the people I grew up around in a new light.

Children need to feel love, safety and belonging. In those refugee families who had lost their roots, there was no sense of belonging. The parents of the forgotten generation of war and post war children never truly felt safe, because their experience had taught them that at any minute they could lose everything. They loved their children, but because they had disconnected from their own emotions, they were often unable to show that love in the way the children would have needed to see it. According to the book, there was a whole generation of post war children who felt lost, many becoming alcoholics or suffering from depression, often feeling like a drifting ship without an anchor.

Most people who had lived through the war, including my grandparents, never talked about it. As a self-preservation mechanism, they buried the whole trauma deep within themselves and desperately tried to create a better life for their children. A life of security. Emotions were not part of the deal. In fact, they were best kept hidden, as allowing them to surface might open up wounds that would be too overwhelming. My grandmother's story was a story of millions. It is estimated that over 14 million people were displaced during the Second World War. Many of them were refugees who would never return to the villages and towns where their families had often lived for hundreds of years. Millions of women were raped by soldiers who themselves had been away from their families and wives for years, who had their own traumas to deal with. Until she died, I did not know my grandmother's story and certainly hadn't realised before reading this book, how common her experience was. For me, my grandmother had always been an old woman with grey hair. I never thought about the fact that my grandparents were once children, teenagers and young lovers with dreams and desires. I never thought about how much unresolved trauma they had buried within themselves since the end of the war.

When I was little, in Soviet occupied East Germany, we would often have Soviet Army convoys pass through our villages. Kilometres of soldiers sitting on open back army trucks, looking out over the wide lands of their occupation, looking lost and grateful for a smile. My grandmother would always say: "Those poor buggers. They are so far from home." I remember cycling out with her to meet them, baskets full of sandwiches strapped to our bicycles, which we would throw up to the soldiers, who happily and gratefully received them. Was this my grandmother's way of practicing forgiveness? She could have reacted with hatred towards Russians or soldiers, but instead she had empathy for them and their own plight. I suppose cooking as a chef in the army canteen, she later in her own life had the opportunity to see the world through the eyes of a soldier. Nothing ever justifies the horrors of war, but understanding other perspectives sometimes makes it a little easier to make your peace with the trauma.

All this work on myself and my family trauma is making me very emotional. I cry a lot, and while this is a healthy release, it also at times feels overwhelming. I learn to put a barrier between my own experiences and those that belong to my grandmother. A barrier that had never existed before. For years, I had imagined being the orphan my grandmother was. I had suffered her story, felt the pain of her rape. Just like the meditation my coach had taken me on to heal my ancestry line had felt totally real, my grandmother's story had been relived time and time again in my own mind. I now realise, how much internal stress this has caused my body. Now I know, that when the body is stressed, it cannot function normally, nor can it heal. My protective bubble allows me to decide what makes it through the outer layer and what I keep away from me. It's like a magic cloak and it helps me to learn to differentiate between my own energies and energies that aren't mine. I am freeing myself from all the trauma that doesn't actually belong to me. By creating a protective barrier, I can observe what happened to me or my ancestors from a safe distance. I can be empathetic, without going through the emotional upheaval. I don't know yet, that becoming an observer of life rather than being entangled in it, is a very important step on a soul's journey of spiritual growth.

It's raining and I sit by the window watching the raindrops fall from the sky. How happy all the plants outside must be about the rain, the elixir of life! It is cleansing and healing. Water can make the most wilted things come to life again. Like the plants outside my window, I am regenerating.

CHAPTER 22
A DAY OF SILENCE

About halfway through the month, there is a day of silence. For twenty four hours, from sunset to sunset, we are not allowed to speak a single word. I wake early, as I do most days. Remembering my childhood as the daughter of a hunter, I decide to go out and take a morning walk in the forest. When I was little, out on early morning hunts with my dad, I used to love making my footsteps inaudible, merging with the pre-dawn silence around me. It was my favourite time of day then, and it still is now. I walk slowly, I become the forest. Each step gently moulds into the soft natural carpet below my feet, a carpet woven in intricate layers of composted leaves. Last autumn's death gifting nutrients to this year's life. The peaceful darkness of the night dawning into the golden waking of another day.

Woodruff grows in patches everywhere along the path, reminding me of stories from my mum's childhood, when my grandmother would make a delicious woodruff syrup, a real treat for a child growing up in a poor post war refugee family. Blackberry bushes to my left form thickets of protection for small animals and birds. The sun creeps higher, sprinkling Mother Nature's concert hall with golden twinkles of light. The symphony orchestra of forest birds has finished tuning their instruments and their concert in is full swing by now, reaching their crescendo as the sun fully rises above the horizon. Ahead of me, on the path is a deer. I'm walking so slowly and quietly it hasn't spotted me yet. It is munching on the dew covered grass that's lining the edges of the path we are both on. An overhanging beech branch becomes my hideout and I watch for what feels like an eternity. Eventually it senses my presence and looks up inquiringly. It looks my way, but either doesn't see me or decides I'm nothing to be scared of. It changes position slightly before going back to munching its breakfast.

This reminds me that it must be nearly seven: time for oil pulling and sauerkraut juice, time for my own breakfast, time to return to my Day of Silence, which could not have started more beautifully. A few days earlier I had spotted a book in the Centre's small library about Spirit Animals. When I return, I look up the meaning of deer. Tribal cultures like the American Indians for instance, used to believe that every encounter, even an animal encounter, happens for a reason and is an exchange of messages. This book helps me decipher the message of my deer. A deer represents inner peace, tranquillity, gentleness, intuition, graceful action and self-awareness. They are certainly all things I am currently working on. Deer have a strong spiritual connection, as they are aware of subtle energies all around them. Interesting. Deer seek refuge within the depths of the forest, where the earth energy is strongest. They are intricately aware of the interconnectedness of everything in their ecosystem. Deer also have a very light, graceful, and quiet presence, their airy element is reflected in their speed, agility, flexibility and intelligence.

According to the book, when a deer crosses our path, it brings awareness to the subtleties of life and allows us to slow down and feel what is happening in our immediate energetic environment. What a beautiful message that totally fits in with what is currently happening to me. I love the idea of animals or plants carrying a message for us. Googling 'spiritual meaning of... fox, squirrel, wood pecker, ant, butterfly or whatever animal crosses our path' is such a great way of feeling connected to our surroundings. Life is so much more fun when everything has meaning, when nothing is a coincidence, when everything is relevant in some way.

Is this utter rubbish? My rational brain kicks into gear every now and again. I imagine my husband laughing at my thoughts and reflections. Are animal or plant encounters truly a message from the universe? I don't care what is real and what isn't real anymore. In fact, my whole idea of reality gets flipped upside down constantly here, and I have totally become used to my world view being dismantled and reassembled in a new way every day. I realise the absurdities of some of the limiting beliefs I have clung onto for years. Beliefs that have made me so ill I no longer wanted to be part of this beautiful world. Who decides what is real and what isn't? Was all my guilt, my shame, my fear real? No. I just wasted lots of energy on negative emotions in the past. What for? I'm not good enough. I'm not working hard enough. I can't possibly sit down before everything is done. No end to the eternal rat race of the twentieth century human experience. Why would I choose to be miserable when I could just as easily choose to be happy?

Allowing for the possibility that I have a choice in all this, is a life changing concept. Could happiness truly be a choice? What if it's not something we need to work hard for, but what if it is always there, waiting for us to tune into, right here, right now, at this very moment? Being able to see the beauty that is everywhere around me makes me feel happy. It makes me happy to think animals are connected to me and carry little messages for me. I smile every time a butterfly flutters by and for the first time in a long time, I feel such gratitude again for being part of this beautiful game called life. There is so much every one of us can be happy about every single day. The flowers smile at us without wanting anything back in return. The rain falls to nourish our Earth and all the innumerable life forms it shelters. We are spinning at a ridiculous speed through the cosmos. How unlikely is the whole idea of life? Yet, here we are!

All these realisations and I haven't even had breakfast yet. Silence is definitely a powerful tool for self-reflection. While a younger version of me would have felt a little apprehensive about today, I feel unfazed. After all, I have become used to not speaking, having spent most of the past year in silence due to my vocal cord growths and operations. While the silence of the last year was not my choice, however, today's silence is a choice. I chose to be here. We all agreed to this Day of Silence. So it feels different. I'm observing myself. Not having to interact with anyone allows me to really watch my emotions and what goes on inside me. I become aware that sitting at the table for breakfast with the others without speaking still triggers me. Interesting. I have learnt to be happy with my own company, but when I am with others, I still feel a need to interact. Why is that? Why do I feel that shared stillness has to be filled with words?

This makes me realise how much I have in the past dominated conversations, filling the silence that would allow people to just be. The silence that might allow quieter people to say something. Silence in a group makes me feel uncomfortable, so I just barge in and talk. Sitting with the others in silence over breakfast, I make a decision: I am going to try chatting less. After all, if a group is together then there are others in the group who can fill the silence if they feel the need. Maybe they don't. Maybe they are quite happy with collective silence and I have been interrupting their peace with my constant chitter chatter. Today, it definitely helps me that we are all in the same boat. The collective agreement makes the silence so much easier. It's a revelation to find out that not speaking is actually okay. Chewing my breakfast in silence makes me taste the food more, the fruit salad is practically exploding on my tongue, a firework of taste sensations. From now on, I promise myself not to feel like I have to fill silences anymore, but to embrace them as something beautiful rather than something awkward.

Given our strict instructions to not utter a single word today, I decide to escape into the forest again after breakfast, spending the rest of the morning walking. Away from people, it will be easier not to speak. I only meet one elderly couple on the way and instead of saying hello I give them a nice broad smile. This is not a new thing for me. After each of my voice operations, I had to have two weeks of total voice rest. So I have gone on dog walks and just smiled at people instead of saying, 'good morning' or 'hello'. As always, I do feel a little weird doing this. The couple, however, are so involved in their own conversation, they don't seem to even notice. They greet me with a smile and walk on. Maybe there is no need to feel awkward about not speaking. Maybe I do need to allow more stillness when I'm with others. Maybe I have been way too self-conscious, way too absorbed in my own uncertainties, way too worried about what other people may think about me. Maybe it is time to finally just be me, not the people pleaser version of me, but just me. Maybe it is okay to chat when I want to chat, and to be silent when I don't want to say anything. Maybe. Maybe I got it all wrong. Maybe I can relearn everything. Maybe I can start looking at the whole world from a different perspective.

I spend the day thinking positive thoughts. Wow, this really works! Beautiful! Just like drugs alter your perception, feeling positive alters everything I look at. Another ray of sunshine tickles my nose, shining brightly through the trees, illuminating the path I choose to follow. I follow my nose, I follow the sun! No plan, no direction, no obligations, no expectations. Thousands of beech leaves twinkle in the golden rays, leading me on to a hidden clearing away from the feet of the usual forest ramblers. It feels wonderfully peaceful here. Just me, the trees, the bushes, and the pathways made by animals. I can see them criss-crossing. A whole network of trails, a parallel forest world existing alongside our human version.

In the afternoon of our Day of Silence, we all meet for a Ho'oponopono ritual. Ho'oponopono means 'to make things right' and is a Hawaiian ritual for forgiveness. According to Ho'oponopono, everything that is our reality is simply an illusion created by our mind. Our mind decides if something is perceived as good or bad, positive or negative. Our mind constantly gives everything around us meaning and makes us interpret the world. Clearly, this is a concept that seems to weave through many cultures and spiritual teachings. Ho'oponopono is an ancestral Hawaiian practice in which people get in touch with their negative emotions, such as anger, and accept the errors of their ways as a valuable part of their soul journey. Anger we feel, mistakes we dwell on, negative energies we carry within us for too long will cause disease. To be healthy, we mustn't hold on to them. Instead of feeling guilty for having negative thoughts, we simply notice them and release them by saying or thinking:

> I love you.
> I'm sorry.
> Please forgive me.
> Thank you.

We meet all negative thoughts and false beliefs with gratitude, love and forgiveness. We show gratitude for what we've learned and feel love for ourselves and everyone around us. In the ancient cultures of Hawaii, people would understand their community as one organism. If someone fell ill, the whole community would need to heal. If someone hurt someone else, there would be no blame. They would heal the whole community, as everyone would take responsibility for their part in what happened. And that part may be, that you didn't notice the pain, desperation or anger of the person who behaved out of line. It is the community's duty to care for and look after each of its members, ensuring everyone's wellbeing. The nature and environment around them would also be seen as part of the community. Everything is one connected organism. I love that way of looking at the world. Nobody is an island, everyone is just one tiny part of a bigger whole.

Later this afternoon, we meet in silence and are taken through a simple but oh-so-powerful ritual of forgiveness. We all have to write down on little pieces of paper, what it is we need to forgive ourselves or others for. I feel the tears welling up and allow them to flow freely. It is so liberating to finally forgive myself for all those years of not looking after my own well-being, for not caring enough for myself. I forgive myself for all the guilt I felt. I forgive myself for all the negative thoughts I allowed myself to think, for all the hours I spent worrying, creating inner stress that prevented my body from healing. For all the years I carried my grandmother's sorrow within me, instead of just allowing myself to fully enjoy life.

We all gather around a fire and one after the other, we burn the pieces of paper. Our pleas for forgiveness go up in smoke. They are taken by the fire to be transformed, to transform us. Fire is the element of transformation, it burns everything to the ground, so something new can arise, like a phoenix from the ashes.

I spend the rest of the afternoon in meditation, doing visualisations and healing myself with Reiki: my ovaries, my womb, my throat. In my mind, I'm creating the life I want to live. Finding my own voice, speaking my truth will be my focus going forward. There is a deep knowing inside me, that if I commit to total honesty with myself and others, to total authenticity whatever situation I find myself in, I will heal. Even though I have spent many months resting my voice, this dedicated day of silence adds yet another layer to my lived experience of self-realisation. I gain a different awareness of myself yet again. I am making peace with my endo dragon and open up to the magic of life again. The ceremonial end to the day, symbolically letting go of what no longer serves me by burning it in the fire, is incredibly transformative and I really do feel lighter afterwards. In the silence of the day, challenges become gifts. In the stillness, many things rise up from within, things I tried to bury, often for years, decades. They drift to the surface to be looked at, to be seen. What I am beginning to understand is that they rise in order to be healed and forgiven. Once this work is done, I am free to be my true self.

FROM ENDO WAR TO INNER PEACE

In the silence, I can hear my inner voice.
In the silence, I find an unknown clarity.
In the silence, I am finally home.

I love you.
I'm sorry.
Please forgive me.
Thank you.

CHAPTER 23
EMOTIONS AS ENERGY

Every day and with every activity we do, we are learning to understand our body as energy. Just like the food we eat and the thoughts we think are energy, our emotions are 'energy in motion'. If we measure people's energy levels when they feel certain emotions, we can actually see the different frequency ranges. Negative emotions like anger, fear, worry, shame and guilt vibrate at a low frequency range, while emotions such as joy, gratitude, love, peace put our cells into high vibrational frequencies. We all use energy language to describe this phenomenon:

> 'I'm feeling low today'
> 'There were good or bad vibes (vibrations) at this party'
> 'S/he is on my wavelength'.

We reference vibrations and use high-low as descriptions for our mood all the time, without knowing that what we are saying is actually true. Each cell in our body vibrates. And our emotions influence the frequency range they vibrate in. The true power of all this positive thinking we have been practicing sinks in. By making myself think positive thoughts, I raise the vibrations in my cells. Apparently, a cell that vibrates in a higher range can activate an inbuilt mechanism for self-healing. A cell vibrating in a lower range loses the power to do this. My rose-tinted glasses go on. From now on, I am going to just focus on the positive. I will not allow anything bad to enter my thoughts. I now get why they want us to see our illnesses as friends. If I regard endometriosis as my enemy, the negative emotions (hatred, worry, anger, grief or fear) will prevent me from activating my body's self-healing power. If I treat endometriosis as my friend, I will stay emotionally in the higher vibrations and in these higher frequencies, healing is at least a possibility.

Apparently, there is also a system of resonance at play. Frequencies of the same range tend to be attracted to each other. If you vibrate high, you attract high ranges. Bad vibes attract bad energy vibrations into your field. So effectively this means, that everything we think, say or feel directly influences our body's ability to heal. Watching and observing every single thought my mind thinks is going to be a colossal task!

All my daily exercises help me do this better and better each day. I am developing awareness, learning how to transform how I word things. I am looking for the learning potential in everything that happens, taking responsibility for my life and my choices. I try to be one hundred percent honest with myself at all times and I am truly becoming aware of my needs. Day after day, week after week, I learn to master the art of positive thinking. Maybe, just maybe, my illnesses are a gift, guiding me towards a long needed change, a springboard into a better life. Could it be possible that I will look back at all these years of pain and agony and be grateful for them one day for having been the catalyst that brought me home to my true self?

Visualisations help me to become aware of the effect of negative or positive mind stories on my body and the way I feel. It is fascinating to witness first hand how contracted and tense a negative thought makes my whole body feel and how much lighter, open and expanded a positive thought makes me feel. The hardest thing is to become aware of the fact 'that I am thinking'. I am so used to my mind rattling on constantly in some inner dialogue and mind chatter, that half the time it happens without me even knowing. Like a hawk, I start to watch and observe my own mind. Meditations help to experience the difference between actively thinking and finding inner stillness. A little trick to stop myself from thinking negative thoughts is to say 'STOP' whenever I become aware of my mind going into the negative or into unnecessary ramblings. For months, I will be saying STOP a lot.

STOP. STOP. STOP. STOP. STOP.

STOP. STOP. STOP.

STOP!

CHAPTER 24
RETURNING HOME

As the days turn into weeks, the end of our four week stay looms. The person returning home feels very different to the person that left, at least internally. Will my husband still love me? Will my son still recognise his mum? I've been so focused on myself and my own healing, that starting to think about others again feels strange.

I am worried. I want to take all the things I have learned and never ever forget them again. I want to take the life I lived for the past four weeks home with me. As the departure day is coming closer, it dawns on me what a colossal task this is going to be: oil pulling, sauerkraut juice, Budwig breakfast, daily coffee enemas, daily bicarbonate soda baths, fresh juices twice a day. Back home, I'm going to have to cook the Budwig meals myself, there will be no professional chefs doing it for me. At least while my voice is still hoarse, I am effectively unemployed and will have the time to nurture myself, to focus on my healing.

'Never ever rely on a man financially. Always make sure you've got skills and can support yourself,' my grandmother's words have lost some of their power over me. There is so much judgement. Growing up, there were no housewives. After the unification, the idea of a woman being a housewife was looked down upon by the women around me, who had been brought up and praised as equal and valuable members of East Germany's workforce. I just have to overcome my own judgement of housewives as something 'less than' and embrace a new perspective. At this point, without a voice, I could no longer work as a teacher; that much was clear.

What would I be able to do without a voice? Data entry? I hate computers! What am I going to do when I get home?

In the stillness of meditation, the message that forms in my head is loud and clear: having invested ten thousand Euros into coming here, having learned everything I learned, it would be ludicrous to go home and not carry on my Budwig routine. So yes: I will return home, become a housewife, rely on my husband's income and heal. However long it will take. I will tell all my clients that I will not go back to teaching. I will put myself first and focus solely on me. Making this decision feels like a massive turning point. In order to do this, I will have to let go of so many of my core beliefs around values, worthiness, the role of women, equality, motherhood, society, expectations. Can I truly just let these core beliefs float away, let them vanish into thin air, when for years they defined how I saw the world? I am still drawn between the old reality I am leaving behind and the new reality waiting to be created. I am thirty nine years old. Can I start again? Would it be possible to reinvent myself?

There is doubt. There is fear of the unknown. There is fear of judgement, my own and that of others. Juxtaposed to this is the experience of the past month. An inner lightness, hope, joy. The promise of a life free from pain. The freedom of just being. Being without thinking. Just me. Without all those beliefs, limitations and expectations. I want that freedom! I long to spread my wings and fly.

I decide it might be a good idea to write a letter to my husband, explaining what I've gone through, what realisations I've had and what my plans are when coming home. I know he's worried. From the few phone calls we have had, I can tell that he is very cautious and doesn't want to pressure me into anything, but he's also a little apprehensive. Who will be returning? Will I still want to be with him? Will he still want to be with me? None of us actually says any of this out loud, but these thoughts hang in the air, like rain clouds gathering mass. Will they pass above our heads or will they burst and leave us drenched? I can't think about us right now. I will focus on me and everything will fall into place one way or another. I love my husband. We will muddle through this and if we don't, it will also be fine. We are not just lovers, but also best friends and I can't see that part ever changing. So for now, I will stop overthinking (Hello mind! STOP!). I am making healing my priority.

My mum has been holding the fort for me at home, running the household. She is my grandmother's daughter and just as strong and capable. There is nobody in the world I would trust more than her to look after my family. I will never be able to find words for how grateful I am that she has not just given me the money to come to the Budwig Centre, but also flown to England for a month to care for my son and husband in my absence. I owe it to her, my son, my husband and most of all to myself to focus on my own healing.

Our last week at the Centre is all about the life we wish to create, the person we would like to be. We all have to write down five things about each person in our group. Five things about how we see them. There is only one rule - the five things have to be something positive. Here is what the others write about me:

Emmie

- Full of humour, happy, honest, creative, quick witted
- Motivating, helpful, creative, open, good energy
- Creative, open, intelligent, good communicator, honest, nature-loving
- Funny (always puts a smile on my face), smart, strong, happy, supportive
- Lovely being, inspiring, ready to help

It is a powerful thing to look at how others see me. We often aren't able to see ourselves the way others do. I self-criticise, I self-judge, and I put myself down all the time. I can find lots of reasons why I am not good enough, strong enough, or courageous enough. I am a master in convincing myself why things wouldn't work or why I wouldn't be successful. To see in black and white how other people perceive me, makes me realise that maybe it was time to start believing in myself a bit more. One of our last afternoon activities is to create a vision board. I absolutely love this! I love being creative anyway, but creating a poster of everything I would like in my new life is such an exhilarating way to spend an afternoon.

> I want to do my Reiki Master Level.
> I want to explore shamanism.
> I want to do yoga every day and practice a head stand.
> I want to go to Scotland, I've never been.
> I want to live in an eco hut in a forest.
> I want to write.
> I want to be an author.
> I want to find some new friends with an interest in spiritual things.
> I want to grow my own vegetables.
> I want to learn about medicinal herbs.

Words, images, merge into each other in a collage of my dreams. At this point, all of it feels like a utopia, a utopia I allow myself to put on paper though. Something significant has changed over the last month: I believe that it is possible for me to create this utopia.

Our final goodbyes are tearful. We all know that even though each of us has been absorbed in their own journey, we will always be connected through our month at the Budwig Centre. The month where we said goodbye to our old life and started to lay the foundations for a new one. Five destinies briefly intertwined at one of the most life changing intersections of our soul journeys. On the last morning, five hopeful souls say goodbye to each other after the most transformative four weeks. I get a lift to the train station from one of my fellow patients. In the station car park we hug.

> "You know, I don't think my month here would have been what it was without you. I don't think we others would have connected the way we did as a group if it hadn't been for you," he says.
>
> "Really?" I am literally gobsmacked to hear him say this.
>
> "Yes, really. You are the one that brought us all together. Thank you!"
>
> "Oh, that's such a lovely thing to say! Thank you! Let's stay in touch!"

We both know we won't stay in touch. The five of us were thrown together to move through a momentous shift in our lives. It is now time to each walk our own path again. Sitting on the train, I think about those last words. Could it really be that I had such an important role in connecting the group? I hadn't been at all aware of it. But actually, looking back now, I realise that this is a skill I have, I had just never thought of it as a skill: I am good at bringing people together, I am good at making people feel included, at creating community. What a nice thought! It feels good to think little, insignificant me has made a difference. It feels good to be valued and to be acknowledged. The train pulls into the airport station: home sweet home, here I come!

CHAPTER 25
STICKING TO MY GUNS

Coming home is a mixed bunch of feelings. Who am I? How much have I changed? Would the people I left notice the monumental shift that had occurred deep within me? What is my life going to be like? I look the same, and in many ways I am still the same person that had left a month earlier. In other ways, I have changed so profoundly, I no longer recognised myself. Big hellos, hugs and smiles. Underneath the outer surface the fear of the unknown is simmering. I can feel it acutely in myself and in my husband. My son, my mum and the dog are just happy to see me again. So many of my beliefs have been turned upside down, dismantled. How am I going to go on from here? I take a deep breath. First steps first. Let's take it slowly. I have been taught a very regimented daily routine and I tell my family that I would like to stick to this routine for at least another two months. Apparently, for the effects of the Budwig protocol to kick in properly, it would take a minimum of three months.

I tell the friends who are covering my language lessons to carry on, as I would not return in a hurry and may not return at all. Deep down, I already know that language teaching isn't what truly fulfils me. I also I have no idea yet, what it is I am meant to do instead. For now, I decide not to think about the future, but to live in the now and to put every ounce of my being into healing my endometriosis. I carry on the Budwig protocol to the letter:

7am	Oil Pulling and Sauerkraut Juice
8am	Budwig Quark Breakfast
8.30am	A 15 Minute Walk
10am	A Freshly Squeezed Juice
12.30pm	Salad and a Light Vegetarian Lunch with Budwig Quark
1pm	Another 15 Minute Walk
1.30	Coffee Enema
4pm	Another Fresh Juice
6pm	A Vegetable Soup for Dinner
6.30pm	A 15 Minute Walk
7pm	A Bicarbonate Soda Bath
10pm	Bed

It is the summer holidays and I slowly ease myself back into home life. Meditations, yoga, gentle walks… sticking to the routine is like a full time job. I don't feel like I can put my husband and son on the same meal routine, so often end up cooking three different meals, although I quickly learn to coordinate and find a common base we can all eat, adding chicken or fish to their diet, while I stick to plant based food. I avoid anything processed; no sugar, wheat, dairy and no alcohol. My diet consists of mainly fruits and vegetables, buckwheat, rice, nuts and seeds. I even keep out grapes and bananas, as their sugar content is very high. Endometriosis lives off sugar. The only dairy I consume is the milk and quark I use to make the Budwig creme. About one month after returning, and two months into my Budwig routine, I can feel a shift. My body feels different. I am still in pain, but the pain has lost its edge. It is a tiny shift, but it is big enough to give me hope. Hope that my Budwig experiment is working. Hope that one day I will be able to live a normal, happy, pain free life again.

September arrives and with it the return to school for my son and the return to routine for my family. My husband agrees that I should focus on my healing journey and not return to work. I finally find the courage to tell my clients that I will not be back. This is massive. Not for them, they got used to their new teachers. But for me. For the first time since becoming a mum, I have no job. I am unemployed. I am a housewife. I rely on my husband's income. I am everything I never wanted to be. I have, however, one significant advantage: the therapy work has made me realise that what I never wanted to be is simply a construct of my own mind, an accumulation of beliefs that I can change at any point. Other people held different beliefs and lived, so it doesn't really actually matter what I believe, as long as what I believe makes me happy. So many of my old beliefs hadn't made me happy, they had made me ill. It was time to let go.

I read. I immerse myself in the books of Dr. Joe Dispenza, Dr. Bruce Lipton, Lynne McTaggart, Esther and Jerry Hicks.[12] Like Dr. Johanna Budwig, these people see the world as energy, as frequency vibrations; and they are merging science and spirituality. I am fascinated and like a starving and thirsty traveller after years in the desert, I devour book after book, my horizon expanding with each one, my old world being replaced by a new world with every word. I am being pushed into a world so much bigger than I could have ever imagined. I feel like a baby, newly arrived in a world infinitely bigger than the world of the womb it believed to be the only reality, until it was pushed through the birth canal. I am discovering a world full of limitless possibilities, a world infinitely bigger than the limited reality I left behind. A world of energy, consciousness, frequency vibrations, meditations, belief patterns, manifestation - a whole new world waiting to be explored.

Six months into my Budwig routine, my symptoms have eased further. The two weeks of excruciating pain I had been in after

---

[12] See Further Reading List at the end of the book for references to book titles.

each period before going to Germany, are down to one week of absolutely manageable pain. I can take ibuprofen and paracetamol and they actually make the pain disappear completely, when beforehand they hadn't really done much. I reduce my daily coffee enemas and bicarbonate soda baths to three times a week. Everything else, I carry on religiously. I meditate every day, I do yoga. My tiredness has gone, and with my newfound energy I start thinking about life beyond Budwig. I remember that I am a qualified Reiki practitioner, having completed my level two Reiki, and decide to turn my son's playroom into a therapy room. Jack has just turned ten and is no longer playing with Lego and Playmobil, but prefers his upstairs room and computer games.

I start seeing clients, first for free, then I charge a small fee. It makes me feel good to earn a little bit of my own money again, even if it's a tiny amount. And it makes me feel absolutely fantastic to give Reiki to people. When channeling Reiki energy to others, I'm healing myself. The energy flows through me and raises my vibrations at least as much as those of my clients. They say time is the greatest healer, and as the weeks turn into months, I can feel myself healing. Meditation becomes a vital part of my journey. Going within, not focusing on anything outside of me is a huge change of perspective for someone who has been a people pleaser all her life. Every morning before I start my day, I listen to my body. What is it I need today? Does my body need rest? Does it need to move? What foods does it want? What do I feel like doing today? What do I want? What do I need right now?

Seven months after returning from Germany, I feel recovered and energized enough to start my Reiki Master training. I know that delving deeper into myself is the key to everything. I know, that it is not outside of me, but in the stillness within that I will find the truth I'm searching for. The Reiki precepts I learned two years previously are no longer some concept I try to remember, they are becoming me. I am becoming them.

> Just for today, I will not worry.
> Just for today, I will not get angry.
> Just for today, I will be honest.
> Just for today, I will be grateful.
> Just for today, I will love myself and every living thing.

In the bathroom of my Master Trainer an indigo fabric wall hanging introduces me to an Apache blessing, I learn off by heart:

> May the sun give you energy by day.
> May the moon softly restore you by night.
> May the rain wash away your worries.
> May the wind blow strength into your being.
> May you walk the Earth and know its beauty every day of your life.

To this day, I say it to myself whenever the need arises, especially on stormy, rainy dog walks. I laugh at the sky. I turn my face towards the clouds or the wind or the rain and recite the blessing in my head. There is no good or bad, there is only the story we tell ourselves. My prayers are being answered. The constant worry I used to feel has almost disappeared completely. My energy levels are returning. I feel strong again. No longer the victim, I am back in the driver seat of my own life. I'm making the rules. I am deciding where my life is heading. I am in charge.

It's not always easy to manoeuvre the new power distribution in the household, but we muddle through it. I communicate. My husband listens and allows me to be. In the past, I was scared of conflict and did everything to avoid it. Now I don't shy away from it. My early attempts at honest communication are a disaster. Since becoming a mom, I had mostly kept quiet to keep the peace, and it's a real hurdle to speak my truth. I have to push through that barrier of fear and the force needed for words to come out makes them come out more fiercely than is healthy. There are arguments, many of them. I recognise the anger I never allowed myself to express. Instead of keeping it hidden inside, I let it out. It takes months to learn to do this lovingly. Success is getting up again and again, when you fail. I become the observer of my own failings. Every one of them becomes an opportunity for learning and growth. Every time I keep quiet, I notice. I observe the people pleaser, I observe the energy getting stuck in my throat. I force myself to overcome my fear of being rejected or disliked. And I learn to speak my truth. Slowly, I'm learning to express myself without judgement, without expectations. I'm learning to meet everything with love, tolerance, wisdom and understanding.

CHAPTER 26
HEALED NATURALLY

The more I work on myself, the more I heal, and the clearer the desire becomes to help others heal themselves, too. I want to be a Budwig Consultant. I want to help women heal from endometriosis. I want to teach others what I have experienced. I want to show them that there is a world of unimaginable possibilities in which healing exists. Not just healing of the body, but healing of the mind, body and spirit. After eighteen months, my endometriosis symptoms have completely disappeared. There is no more pain, no more fatigue, no heaviness in my thighs, no clawing pains in my left buttock. My periods are four to five days long instead of seven to ten. The blood is a beautifully clear red, no longer the dark, brownish smelly mass I was excreting before. I experience something I have never, ever experienced: totally pain free periods. From when I got my periods at the age of eleven, they have always been painful. Now, I find myself going to the toilet, surprised that I've started bleeding. There is no tightness two to three days before the bleeding starts, no cramping, no tummy ache, no lower back pain. Nothing. I can go to the gym on the day of my period. It is just another day like any other, the only difference is, I'm bleeding.

I have found my holy grail. I want to scream out into the world: Endometriosis can be healed! I join endometriosis Facebook groups and forums, trying to connect with women who suffer like I did. I can help you! I barge in with all my wisdom, all my enthusiasm, all my passion for healing. And I fall flat on my face.

Who do you think you are, telling us this incurable disease can be healed?

How dare you suggest that the illness is due to my beliefs and lifestyle!

How dare you say I am responsible for my illness!

How dare you!

How dare you!

How dare you!

I'm not prepared for the barrage of social media onslaught I get. I feel awful. Here I am, trying to help, and now I find myself being attacked. I retreat. I ponder. I analyse my word choice, the energy in my posts. How am I being misunderstood like this? My advice comes from a place of love, yet is turned into disdain and hatred. I reach out to my former consultant to let her know about the Budwig protocol and that it cured me, that there is another way, an alternative to surgery, painkillers and suffering. I contact various endometriosis self-help groups, trying to share my story to give hope to others. Nobody is interested. 'It's great that this worked for you, but endometriosis is an incurable chronic illness. You are a miracle. This cannot be replicated. Good luck!' That's the nice version of NO I get from whichever direction I turn to. My VOICE OF REASON expected, that people would not believe. I was sceptical as well, before I started on this journey, so however much it hurts to be rejected, I understand. However, LITTLE VOICE has grown courageous over the past months and will not give in. I research how to become a Budwig Consultant. There are a couple of courses available, but you have to be a doctor or therapist to do the Budwig training. I'm neither. Yet.

VOICE OF REASON: "Leave it. You've healed yourself. This is what you wanted. In fact, you've achieved way more than you ever thought was possible. You just wanted to get to the point where you could manage the pain until menopause, when your periods will stop anyway. You now have no symptoms. None whatsoever. Just be happy with that."

LITTLE VOICE (*with strength*): "But I feel this deep inner desire to share my knowledge, to share my experience."

VOICE OF REASON: "You are forty, for goodness sake! Your training has been as a linguist… language teacher… translator. You can't just start completely from scratch and reinvent yourself at forty, you know."

LITTLE VOICE: "Says who?"

VOICE OF REASON: "Society. Convention. Reason. It's a ridiculous idea!"

LITTLE VOICE: "Ok. Mmh… I guess I don't really want to go back to the very beginning, start all over again… but I've got several degrees. I'm reasonably intelligent. I think I can do this. And I've got all that lived experience to draw on now. I know I can do this. Ok, let's do some research…"

[*LITTLE VOICE gets up and is surprised by how tall she is. Shoulders back, head up. Go. She moves forward, self-propelled by her own determination.*]

FROM ENDO WAR TO INNER PEACE

THE END (or the beginning of a new journey)

EPILOGUE

In 2016, I had hit rock bottom and realised I needed to change my life. Rediscovering Dr. Johanna Budwig's teachings and going to the Budwig Centre in Germany was the beginning of my healing journey from endometriosis. I'm writing these final pages in 2025. After just eighteen months of living the Budwig protocol, I was totally free of any endometriosis symptoms and had achieved more than I had ever dared to hope for. My own disbelief reflected that of my environment: it seemed too good to be true. Maybe, it was only a short-term illusion? Maybe symptoms would return eventually?

I am now forty eight years old and my periods still arrive each month as regular as clockwork. The early menopause I had once hoped for, hasn't materialised yet. Today, I greet my periods as a valued, welcome and sacred part of being a woman. Am I healed? I sometimes feel our society is scared of the possibility of healing. We are surrounded by chronic illnesses, our cancers go into remission. I allow myself to use the word healing, as I believe it is important for all of us to open up to the possibility of true healing. Our beliefs create our reality. If we don't belief that healing is possible, how are we going to achieve it? In my opinion, chronic illnesses can be healed, and I am not the only one who has experienced this. There are healing journey books and stories of pretty much every illness that exists on this planet. Do we need more proof than the lived experience of so many of us?

There are a few things I would like anyone setting out on their own healing journey to be aware of. Healing, like life, has its ups and downs. Don't give up believing in yourself. There are periods where you will feel stagnation, or you might even sometimes feel you're going backwards. As humans, we do have a limited awareness of what is happening in the body and what processes are involved in healing. Trust. Listen to your body. Keep on taking your next step. You will succeed. Often just before a breakthrough, it feels like a breakdown. Remember how my grandmother in her story said, whenever she felt like giving up, help came from somewhere? That's been my experience, too. So when you do feel down, in despair, disheartened and you start doubting yourself and your journey, try to rest, observe and trust. Usually a period like this is followed by your next breakthrough and help will come from the most unexpected of places.

I have certainly learned that my symptoms are a direct result of my lifestyle choices. After I got better, I experimented. What would happen if I stopped eating the Budwig Diet? If I allowed my stress levels to increase again? My body reacts to all sorts of environmental factors and I am not separate from what happens around me or within me. I've taken the diet experiments to different levels and even lived a year as a raw vegan. While I don't follow the Budwig protocol strictly anymore, I do follow its core teachings in principle to this day. Flaxseed oil and flaxseeds form part of my diet, together with nuts and seeds. I still like the quark mixture, even though I don't eat it every day. I eat a mainly vegetarian diet, but might very occasionally eat a little white meat or fish. Whenever I do, I can feel the difference in my energy levels. Animal protein takes a lot longer to be digested and I feel much heavier and less energetic than I do when I stick to a plant based diet. I listen to my body and trust that it knows best what it needs. For me, white sugar and white flour are the biggest triggers for an increase in pain. Pain won't occur immediately, it's perfectly fine to eat whatever I fancy, but if I don't eat healthily for two to three months, I can feel a tightness in my tummy again, I feel bloated and my energy levels drop significantly. These days, I no longer wait three months, the minute I feel any of these symptoms, I simply return to a healthy lifestyle and the symptoms disappear.

I used to get pains in my left buttocks, going down my left leg, which I always interpreted as endometriosis pain. I have since discovered, that they are actually a symptom of not moving enough. When I had endometriosis, I would spend whole days lying down or sitting, too tired and exhausted to move. Once I started healing and my energy returned, I began to exercise and I realised how important movement actually was for my body's wellbeing. The more I exercised, the more energetic I felt. Even today, whenever I sit a lot, I can feel a pain – albeit a lot less intense – in the same area of my buttocks where it used to hurt when I suffered from endometriosis. When I describe these pains, it's important to say that they are nothing like they were. It's a faint memory, a cotton wool version of the endometriosis pain that once was. But it serves as a reminder to move, to go to the gym, take a walk or do some yoga.

Pain is also a good indicator of my stress levels. I usually have no pain at all when I get my periods now. But if for whatever reason my stress levels are up, I get what most women would know as pre-menstrual syndrome (PMS). I would know my period was on its way: a little tension, some muscle pulling, maybe feeling a bit less energetic; I might feel a bit bloaty around the time of ovulation. All these symptoms disappear again, if I don't stress. I know, that if I want no symptoms at all, all I have to do is meditate every day, exercise regularly and eat a healthy vegetarian or plant based diet. In my opinion, this is a very low price to pay for a happy, pain free life. And not only does it keep endometriosis pain at bay, it helps prevent all sorts of other diseases as well, and it's good for Mother Earth, the beautiful planet we live on. Who doesn't like a win win?

After I healed, I had an incredible desire to share my knowledge with other women who suffered from endometriosis. I wanted to become a Budwig Consultant, but in order to complete the training in Germany, I had to be a therapist or doctor. At the time, I was neither. If there is something you wish to do, follow your heart and believe that you can achieve anything. At the 3E Centre, we were told that our time there would be the start of a new life, and it truly has been for me. I have totally reinvented myself. I retrained as a Health & Life Coach, qualified as a Budwig Advisor, trained in Emotional Freedom Technique (EFT), Matrix Reimprinting, Shamanism and I am a Reiki Master Teacher. None of this would have even been on my radar back in 2016. I facilitate drum circles and have even become a natural beekeeper. If anyone had told me back in 2016 what my life would look like in 2025, I would have laughed and thought it was impossible to get where I am now.

I was lucky enough to have the money to go to Germany, to retrain, to stay at home and focus on my healing. Most people will not have this luxury. Writing this book and running twelve week endometriosis programmes are my way of sharing my knowledge, so what helped me can help others at a fraction of the price I paid. In my experience, the programme I teach today works for those willing to make changes to their lives and their beliefs. You have to be prepared to let go of what no longer serves you, in order to make room for something new to come in.

I love when things are not random, when there is a process behind something. A process that you can learn, understand and apply. I hope the Budwig Protocol outlined in this book will help other women on their own healing journey. Be aware, however, that diet and detox make up for only twenty percent of your healing, eighty percent is down to healing your limiting beliefs and reducing stress in your life.

During my healing journey of self-discovery I thought I was beginning to understand the thing we call 'life'. Today I realise, that maybe there is nothing to understand, but everything to surrender to. I have learned to embrace the unknown. I try to follow my heart without fear. If I feel fear, I know exactly that the fear simply masks my next growth step and I go towards it. American academic, author and podcaster Brené Brown has coined the sentence "Feel the fear and do it anyway" and I fully embrace this at all times. So far, overcoming my fears has led me to my greatest fulfilment and happiness.

Nowadays, if I get triggered by something or someone, I clear my energy field using the Ho'oponopono ritual, EFT tapping or Shamanic Journeying. There is a wealth of energy healing modalities out there, the universe will guide you to the one that's right for you. Just be open for the signs. They might come in the form of an email, an advert, a friend's comment or suggestion, a book, a podcast – whichever way it is brought to your attention, go and explore whatever you feel drawn to. There is a whole world out there, beyond the physical reality, waiting to be discovered! A trigger is simply the universe's way of showing me what still needs healing in me. Whatever is outside of me, is just a mirror that allows me to see myself. When everything is in me, I am no longer a victim of circumstance. I am the one with the power to heal myself.

If you want to play the game of 'Life on Earth', you have to play by the rules of the game or at least know what those rules are so you can manipulate them in your favour. As you awaken to a truer, more authentic version of yourself, you realise that you can stop playing everyone else's game and create your own. I'm done playing by other people's rules, especially if they are rules that do not empower me. I'm done being told by the outside world who or what I am supposed to be. I'm ready to be the best version of me I can be today.

Is this the end of my story? No, but it is the end of my endometriosis story. I am no longer an endo warrior, but have found my inner peace. I carry on walking my path. I help women who suffer from endometriosis as well as anyone with a chronic illness willing to walk their soul path. I hold space for people to find the stillness that allows us to connect with our true selves. I have worked through a long list of limiting beliefs and have proven to myself that the seemingly impossible is possible. I have unknown the known, and embraced the unknown. I open my eyes every morning and welcome limitless possibilities rather than countless limiting certainties. I have become deeply spiritual and this connection to something greater than us gives me the courage and strength to carry on living my life with immense joy and gratitude for whatever unfolds next. I wholeheartedly belief that true healing means healing mind, body and spirit.

I know that my voice is going to get better and that it will be my guide on the next stage of my soul journey. I may not have found the missing puzzle piece for the laryngeal papillomatosis yet, but I surrender to the process. I follow my intuition and the voice that speaks from within. While my physical voice remains hoarse, albeit painless, I still have healing to do for myself, my ancestors and the collective. I'm okay with that. The divine and its timings are always perfect. So who am I in my limited humanness not to trust it?

I know from my endometriosis experience that once I find what works, healing will happen. The voice sits energetically in the throat chakra area, which is all about speaking and expressing my truth. Writing this book has been part of my voice healing journey. Thank you, dear reader, for making it this far with me. There are three things I have learned: Never give up hope, trust your journey and surrender! Everything is in me, just as it is in you. And everything just wants to be loved.

HEALING

Healing happens on the inside,
Healing happens in your sleep,
Healing happens when you allow it,
Healing happens and is yours to keep.

Healing happens to believers,
Healing happens when you trust,
Healing happens when you allow it,
Healing happens 'cause it must.

Healing happens, each soul knows it,
Healing happens, when we laugh,
Healing happens when you allow it,
Healing happens when you embrace your path.

APPENDICES

APPENDIX 1
ENDOMETRIOSIS - A SUBCONSCIOUS FEAR OF PREGNANCY

My original manuscript had a part three, which was all about what happened after the healing, but I decided to shorten this to the epilogue. In my EFT training I came across the idea of 'Endometriosis as a subconscious fear of pregnancy.' This very much resonated with me and has become a belief pattern I always watch out for when I work with women today. So I felt it important to include this chapter nonetheless. It's not always relevant, but I'd say in eighty percent of endometriosis clients, this features in some form.

Endometriosis as a subconscious fear of pregnancy. This statement takes wing and flutters in the air, syllable after syllable it weaves itself into the neurological synapses of my brain. One tiny sentence, uttered in passing by one of the EFT teachers on my training course. As it hits my neurons, it dissolves the fog of unawareness. Rattle, rattle, rattle. My brain has been set in motion. A fear of pregnancy? Something resonates. I think of all the women with endometriosis who desperately wish for a baby. It's not a conscious fear of pregnancy. It's something much deeper, a subconscious belief.

I look at my own story. Yes! I can see it! I had always had painful periods, but the pain started getting worse and becoming what I would now distinctly recognise as that excruciating endometriosis pain, when Jack was about two years old. All the mummy friends around me were starting to talk about second babies. I had always wanted two children. In fact, one of my best childhood friends had been an only child, and I never ever wanted to have an only child.

Just thinking about the possibility of a second child, however, would put me into inner conflict: David was already the happy father of two children. He didn't really want another one. Twenty four years older than me, he felt he had done his service to humankind and procreated, it was time to enjoy life.

> David: 'I'm very happy with the two I've got. I couldn't imagine going through it all again.'
>
> Me: 'I want children. I love you, but not having children for you is a sacrifice I'm not prepared to make. I'm 26 now. I know, that at 42, 45, I would regret not having them and I would resent you and that would destroy our relationship. So if you're sure you definitely don't want any more kids, I accept your choice and respect your honesty. But then I cannot stay with you.'
>
> David: 'Mmh, well, if the choice is a life without you or a life with you, but also with another child, then I'll choose the life with you and the child.'

This is the essence of a conversation I had with David a good three years before I became a mum. I have always been very practical when it comes to big life decisions. I had always wanted a child before I was thirty. If I had to leave David to meet the potential father of that child, I'd need three years to get to the point in a new relationship where we'd be ready for a child. So twenty six was the right time to have this conversation; my cut off point. By this point, we had been together for six years. We knew, our child wouldn't be born until a few years later. Maybe that helped David to say yes back then. In any case, in my own mind and understanding, Jack had been our compromise. David, who wanted no more children. Me, who wanted two children. The fair compromise was to have one.

At thirty two, when thoughts of a second child kept continuously creeping into my mind, the possibility of David agreeing to another was zero, at least in my head. So I didn't even dare to ask the question. At least not properly. I made little comments to test the waters. But the reply to those always confirmed what I believed: David would not want a fourth offspring.

'Endometriosis is a subconscious fear of pregnancy.' I look back at my early thirties. Over the moon as the mother of my boy, thoughts constantly wandering to the second child I would never have, I even asked God to make it my 'fault' and not David's that we have no more children. I was too scared I would one day hold it against him and it would break us. If responsibility for not having a second child lay with me, I could live with it. I could live with blaming myself. I didn't want to get to a point where I would be blaming my husband. What tricks our minds play on us! What absolute masters of self-sabotage we are, as humans!

God heard my wishes and complied. The universe always gives us what we want. Be careful what you wish for! I got endometriosis and with that the empty, barren womb I had asked for. Between the ages of thirty two and thirty nine, exactly the period of my endometriosis years, I would be scared every month that I might be pregnant. Every month, my period pain would arrive and there would be a little part of me that was relieved: not pregnant. For reasons mentioned earlier, I had chosen not to go on the contraceptive pill after Jack was born. We used natural forms of contraception: avoiding sex or using condoms on those four or five critical days of ovulation and just hoped for the best. But every month, I felt this fear of pregnancy towards the end of my cycle.

In my coaching practice, I have encountered this subconscious fear of pregnancy in many disguises. I have met women who had traumatic childhoods; by not becoming a parent themselves, they protect the unborn child from having to go through what they went through. I met women who had painful first pregnancies and protected themselves from going through this experience again by developing endometriosis and becoming infertile. There were women in arranged marriages, who simply did not want a child with the husband they don't truly love. Younger women, who refuse to fulfil the destiny of wife and mother their culture envisages for them.

Numerous other subconscious 'fear of pregnancy beliefs' exist. It is quite incredible how many variations I come across, working with women suffering from endometriosis. *Life will stop being fun, once children come along. I love my independence. I will never be a good mother. I knew as a child, I would never have children. I never wanted children.* The subconscious beliefs preventing us from becoming mothers are as varied and as individual as the women who suffer with endometriosis. The essential core belief pattern that underlies all these variants is a subconscious fear of becoming a mother. A fear of becoming a creator of life, a fear of creating the life you truly want.

I know this will be hard for some women to read. Many of us endo warriors want nothing more than to be a mother. It is really, really important to understand that this fear of pregnancy is not something you will consciously be aware of. It will be lurking somewhere in the unfathomable depth of your subconscious. Endometriosis is a disease that manifests in the womb, the very space of creation. The sacral chakra harbours life's pleasures, life's joy – it is the place from where we create: literally, and metaphorically. If you have endometriosis (or any other illness that affects the sacral chakra area), ask yourself:

> Where am I not creating the life I truly want to live?
> Where do I lack pleasure in my life?
> Where do I lack joy?

Where am I not living my passion?
Where am I not expressing my creativity?

Then do whatever it is you need to do to remedy this lack. I promise you, it'll be your path to healing.

> **The best book on belief patterns behind illnesses:**
>
> Metaphysical Anatomy. Your Body is Talking, Are You Listening? Evette Rose, 2012.

APPENDIX 2
FIGHT OR FLIGHT - THE HUMAN STRESS RESPONSE

While I had experimented with dietary changes before I discovered the Budwig approach, learning about stress and how to switch off the release of stress hormones into the blood stream is possibly the most important lesson I have learned on my healing journey. To eliminate stress from our life, we need to understand what the stress response is and why it is such an integral part of our body system.

We have two nervous systems: the parasympathetic and the sympathetic nervous system. The sympathetic nervous system is responsible for the stress response, otherwise known as 'fight-flight'. The parasympathetic system controls and manages pretty much everything else: cell healing, digestion, absorption of nutrients, and elimination of toxins. It's what's often referred to as the 'rest & digest, feed & breed' response. The two systems cannot be switched on at the same time. If stress is on, all other processes come to a halt until the stress response is switched off, when all normal bodily functions resume. Consequently, in stress or fight-flight mode, our body cannot heal and restore.

The stress response is a vital survival mechanism programmed into us. As humans, we have evolved quite quickly compared to other species on this planet that have been around for millions of years. The stress response is an ancient programme that was originally put into our bodily system to deal with situations that were an actual threat to our survival. Imagine being confronted by a bear or tiger. There are two options: fight the animal or run away as fast as you can (fight-flight). In such situations, which in the past would have been very rare, stress hormones are released into our blood stream, triggering chemical reactions that ensure all the energy available in the body is sent immediately into our muscles. This makes total sense, as it's our muscles that will make us run away faster or deliver stronger punches against a supposed predator.

So the stress response as such is actually a really useful thing. It has ultimately been designed to ensure our survival in extreme situations. As it is supposed to be triggered in life or death scenarios only, it also makes sense that while we run away or fight for our life, anything else in the body that requires energy is switched off. After all, if the tiger catches and kills you, it doesn't really matter if you've digested your breakfast properly or kept your hormonal balance. As an ancient mechanism, this stress response hasn't had time yet to evolve and adapt to our modern lifestyles, especially the fast paced technology driven expansion we have experienced in the past thirty years.

Take a moment to reflect on what stresses you. Are you constantly thinking, constantly rushing, constantly active, constantly exhausted. In our current society, even having a cup of coffee or tea has become a thing many of us do on the go. Sitting down and resting has almost become a sign of weakness. I certainly felt I had to be constantly busy to feel accepted and valued in my surroundings. Judging by the people walking around cradling takeaway coffee cups and eating their sandwiches on the go, I don't think I am an exception. I believe, that the vast number of modern chronic illnesses are the direct result of our daily lives being too stressful. When we get ill, our general approach is to surgically remove the problem, pop a pill and get back to normal as quickly as possible. If our body's regulatory system cannot work properly when the stress mode is switched on, is it any wonder that illnesses become chronic?

Meditation and mindfulness exercises are a great way to gain that awareness. The easiest way to stop the release of stress hormones into the blood stream, is deep breathing. Just ninety seconds of deep breathing are enough to send a signal to the brain that all is well in the world and there is no further need for stress hormones to be released. I cannot stress enough, just how important deep breathing is as a mechanism to switch off the release of stress hormones and recalibrate the body into that sense of inner calm, so healing can take place. To get you started, I have included some very simple breathing exercises here. I suggest, however, you find a local breath work course to deepen your practice.

HOW TO SWITCH OFF THE STRESS RESPONSE

3 EASY BREATHING TECHNIQUES

5-4-7 BREATH
Stand or sit still, completely focus on your breath. Now count to five as you inhale, hold your breath for a count of four, and exhale for a count of seven. Repeat for at least 90 seconds, or as long as it takes to feel calm.

WARM – COLD BREATH
Stand or sit still, completely focus on your breath. Breathe in through your nose and feel the cold air going up your nostrils. Breathe out through your nose and feel the warm air coming out of your nostrils. Keep repeating while focusing on nothing but the temperature in your nostrils: inhale cold, exhale warm. Repeat for at least 90 seconds, or as long as it takes to feel calm.

BOX BREATHING
Imagine drawing a rectangular box with your breath. Start on the top left corner of the box. As you inhale, you draw an imaginary line from left to right, you hold your breath as you draw a line from the top right corner of the box down. Exhale drawing a line from right to left, hold your breath while drawing a line back to the starting point. See the box below: the arrows show you the direction of your breath. Repeat for at least 90 seconds, or as long as it takes to feel calm.

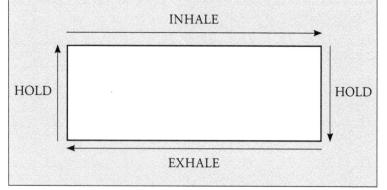

APPENDIX 3
HEALING THE DIVINE FEMININE

As I am delving deeper into the emotional, spiritual and subconscious realms of my being, I become aware of another aspect hidden in my endometriosis: the loss of my feminine power. The power of the feminine is to create. It is the women of this world who create new life. The amount of female illnesses that affect the sacral chakra area, the sexual organs, the reproductive system is a reflection of how far removed from our feminine power many of us are. Looking back at my mum's story, my grandmother's story, looking back at the women I had around me when I grew up, they were all strong women, but every single one of them felt disempowered. Forced to live a life so much smaller than what they would have been capable of. Their job was to keep others happy, not to keep themselves happy.

For centuries, a woman openly expressing her sexuality and desires would be called a slut. For centuries, women were allowed to be the wife of powerful men, but seldom powerful themselves. Where are the stories of the powerful women in our history books? Cleopatra, Jeanne d'Arc? *Behind every man is a strong woman.* Why do we have to be behind the man? We are collectively all working on re-establishing balance in the energy system and bringing back the power of the divine feminine. The 21 century is changing perceptions we have collectively held for centuries. It is down to each of us to embody our divine feminine power within us.

For so many years, I hated being a girl, I hated being a woman. I hated feeling less worthy, less able, less heard, less accepted, less clever. Not just because it put me at a disadvantage, but because I knew it wasn't true. I knew I was just as able as any man I had ever met. Yet, here was a whole society who saw the feminine as weak. Women who did make it into the men's domain of power only got there if they were like the men. The cost for being accepted was to leave your femininity behind. At the same time, men had to be strong, weren't allowed to cry or show emotions and were seen as weak if they did so. In the energy view of the world, everything is created in equal measure of feminine and masculine energies. They are two opposing forces that play with each other and in their playfulness they create the life we see. Each human has these feminine and masculine energies in equal measure within them. They have nothing to do with being a man or a woman, they are merely energetic forces within us all.

The feminine energies are receptive, nurturing, loving, caring, intuitive. They embrace stillness and growth, their focus is on being. The masculine energies are active, moving, forceful, strong, courageous, their focus is on doing and achieving. What we need to understand is that these energies are within us in equal measure, regardless of our gender. We have access to both of them and we ourselves should decide when we tap into which force, i.e. when we are nurturing, loving or caring, or when a situation demands strength, courage, or drive.

Our collective healing is under way every second of every day. 'Me Too' has brought more balance into the power divide. Women are finding their voices, men are reconnecting with their emotions, embracing the softer aspects of their feminine essence. Today, men are allowed to talk about their feeling in a way they haven't been for centuries. I feel optimistic about us as humans finding the balance we so long for. I am convinced that when we do find this balance, the dis-eases will disappear. They are only here to show us the way, to make us aware that our systems need to be recalibrated. Collectively, we will heal when each one of us heals individually, healing always starts within ourselves.

So here is my plea to you, dear reader: Start working on yourself today. Start loving yourself today. Awaken to the power within you. Each of us working on ourselves, stepping into our true power, believing in ourselves, creating the life of our dreams, will change the world we collectively create and share.

GLOSSARY A-Z

Acupuncture: Acupuncture is a treatment derived from ancient Chinese medicine. Fine needles are inserted at certain sites in the body for therapeutic and preventative purposes. (https://www.nhs.uk/conditions/acupuncture/)

Bowel resection: A bowel resection is a surgery to remove any part of the bowel. (https://www.webmd.com/colorectal-cancer/bowel-resection)

Bowen Therapy: Bowen Therapy is an alternative type of physical manipulation. It involves gentle rolling motions across the muscles, tendons and fascia. Distinctive pauses help the body to reset itself.

Cervix: The cervix is a small canal that connects the uterus and vagina. It allows fluids to leave and enter the uterus. During childbirth, the cervix widens so that a baby can be born. (https://my.clevelandclinic.org/health/body/23279-cervix)

Chakra: Chakra is the Sanskrit word for wheel or cycle and refers to energy centres in the body. There are seven main centres, each on is linked to specific organs and emotional states. (https://en.wikipedia.org/wiki/Chakra)

Dark field microscopy: Dark field microscopy uses a special microscope and describes an illumination technique used to enhance the contrast in unstained samples. It is a very simple, yet effective technique and well suited for uses in involving live and unstained biological samples, such as a smear from a tissue culture or individual, water-borne, single-celled organisms. Considering the simplicity of the setup, the quality of images obtained from this technique is impressive. (https://en.wikipedia.org/wiki/Dark-field_microscopy)

Endometrioma: Endometriomas are usually benign growths, most often found in the ovary, often called chocolate cysts. They form dark fluid filled cysts, which can vary greatly in size. The fluid inside the cyst is thick, dark, old blood, giving it a chocolate-like appearance. (https://en.wikipedia.org/wiki/Emdometrioma)

Endometriosis: Endometriosis is where cells similar to those in the lining of the womb (uterus) grow in other parts of the body. Endometriosis usually grows in areas around the womb, such as the ovaries and fallopian tubes. It can also affect organs such as the bladder and bowel. (https://www.nhs.uk/conditions/endometriosis/)

Fibrosis is also known as scarring. It is uncontrolled wound healing in which connective tissue replaces normal parenchymal tissue to the extent that it goes unchecked, leading to considerable tissue remodelling and the formation of permanent scar tissue. Repeated injuries, chronic inflammation and repair are susceptible to fibrosis.
(https://en.wikipedia.org/wiki/Fibrosis#:~:text=Fibrosis%2C%20also%20known%20as%20fibrotic,formation%20of%20permanent%20scar%20tissue)

GnRH (Prostap): Stands for gonadotropin-releasing hormone and is involved in making the male and female sex hormones testosterone, oestrogen and progesterone. Prostap is simply the brand name of a chemically produced version of these hormones. (https://my.clevelandclinic.org/health/body/22525-gonadotropin-releasing-hormone).

Homeopathy: Homeopathy is a type of complementary or alternative medicine that's based on the use of highly diluted substances, which practitioners claim can cause the body to heal itself.
(https://www.nhs.uk/conditions/homeopathy/)

Hysterectomy: A hysterectomy is the surgical procedure to remove the womb from a woman's body.
(https://www.nhs.uk/conditions/hysterectomy/)

Iridology: Iridology is an alternative medicine technique which claims that patterns, colours, and other characteristics of the eye's iris can be examined to determine information about a patient's systemic health. Practitioners use iris charts, which divide the iris into zones that correspond to specific parts of the body. The eyes are seen as "windows" into the body's state of health.
(https://en.wikipedia.org/wiki/Iridology)

Laparoscopy: Laparoscopy is a type of keyhole surgery used to diagnose and treat conditions. It allows a surgeon to use only small cuts and a camera for procedures inside the tummy or pelvis.
(https://www.nhs.uk/conditions/laparoscopy/)

Ovarian: relating to the ovaries.

Ovary: The ovary (from Latin *ovarium* or egg, nut) is a gonad in the female reproductive system that produces eggs. When released, an egg travels from the ovaries through the fallobian tubes into the uterus. There is an ovary on the left and right side of the body. The ovaries are endocrine glands, secreting various hormones that play a role in the menstrual cycle and fertility.
(http://en.wikipedia.org/wiki/Ovary)

Papimi machine: A special machine developed by Dr. Pappas, which is based on the principle of ion-induction and ranked among the large family of PEMP (pulsed electromagnetic field) devises. It produces electromagnetic oscillations which influence the entire organism or targeted areas of application. www.papimi.com

Peritonial Excision: The surgical removal of the peritoneum (see below).

Peritonium: The peritoneum is a membrane, a sheet of smooth tissue that lines the abdominal cavity and surrounds the abdominal organs. It pads and insulates the organs and holds them in place and secretes a lubricating fluid to reduce friction when they rub against each other.
https://my.clevelandclinic.org/health/body/22894-peritoneum

Pouch of Douglas: The pouch of Douglas (rectovaginal pouch, or cul-de-sac) is the extension of the peritoneum into the space between the back wall of the womb and the rectum in the human female.
(https://en.wikipedia.org/wiki/Rectouterine_pouch) [Author's note: it's a tiny empty space between the womb and the anus.]

Retroflexed uterus: A retroverted (or retroflexed) uterus is a common condition that describes how your uterus sits within your pelvis. A retroverted, or tilted, uterus is when your uterus is tilted backward toward your spine. It doesn't cause any serious health problems but can cause discomfort during sex and painful menstruation.
(https://my.clevelandclinic.org/health/diseases/23426-retroverted-uterus)

TCM (Traditional Chinese Medicine): TCM is a system of medicine that aims to prevent or heal disease by maintaining or

restoring yin-yang-balance. It is one of the oldest medical systems, which includes acupuncture and Chinese herbal remedies that date back over 2200 years.
(htpp://www.britannica.com/science/traditional-chinese-medicine)

Trans fats: Trans-fatty acids are unsaturated fatty acids that come from industrial or natural sources. Their use has increased considerable in the past few years. According to the World Health Organisation, trans fats clog arteries and increase the risk of heart attacks. They can be found in margarine, fried food, baked goods, meat and dairy.
(https://www.who.int/news-room/fact-sheets/detail/trans-fat#:~:text=Trans%20fat%2C%20or%20trans%2Dfatty,of%20heart%20attacks%20and%20deaths.)

Uterus: The uterus or womb is the organ in the reproductive system of women that accommodates the embryonic or foetal development of one or more fertilized eggs until birth. The uterus is a hormone-responsive sex organ.
(https://en.wikipedia.org/wiki/Uterus)

Vagina: The vagina is the elastic, muscular reproductive organ of the female genital tract. It extends from the vulva to the cervix.
(https://en.wikipedia.org/wiki/Vagina)

Warburg effect: In oncology, the Warburg effect is the observation that most cancer cells use aerobic glycolysis, a fermentation process, for energy generation rather than the mechanisms used by non-cancerous cells.
(https://en.wikipedia.org/wiki/Warburg_effect_(oncology))

Womb: see uterus above

BIBLIOGRAPHY & FURTHER READING

I am a bookworm and have read hundreds of books on self-development, spiritual development and energy healing. Those books that were most relevant to my endometriosis healing journey are listed below.

On Endometriosis

Dian Shepperson Mills & Michael Vernon: Endometriosis. A Key to Healing and Fertility Through Nutrition. Thorsons, 2002. (There is a new edition now available from 2023).

Wendy K. Laidlaw: Heal Endometriosis Naturally without Painkillers, Drugs, or Surgery. Create Space Independent Publishing, 2015.

Wendy K. Laidlaw also has a very good Endometriosis Podcast.

On The Budwig Protocol

Dr. Johanna Budwig: Flax Oil as a True Aid Against Arthritis, Heart Infarction and Cancer. Apple Publishing, 1994. (Add Publisher and year)

Dr Johanna Budwig: Oel-Eiweiss Kost. Sensei, 2013.

A good English website about the protocol is www.budwig-diet.co.uk

On Physics and Quantum Physics

Albert Einstein: The World As I See It. Snowball Publishing, 2014.

Albert Einstein: Relativity. The Special and The General Theory. BN Publishing, 2010.

Carlo Rovelli: Seven Brief Lessons on Physics. Penguin, 2016.

Carlo Rovelli: Reality Is Not What it Seems. The Journey to Quantum Gravity. Penguin, 2017.

Chad Orzel: How to Teach Quantum Physics to Your Dog. Oneworld Books, 2010.

John Polkinghorne: Quantum Theory: A Very Short Introduction. Oxford University Press, 2002.

Stephen Hawking: A Brief History of Time. From Big Bang to Black Holes. Penguin, 2016.

Stephen Hawking: The Theory of Everything. The Origin and Fate of The Universe. Phoenix Books, 2008.

On Generational Trauma (in German):

Sabine Bode: Die vergessene Generation. Die Kriegskinder brechen ihr Schweigen. Klett, 2015.

On Energy Healing, Meditation and The Power of Belief:

Dr. Bruce Lipton, Steve Bhaerman: Spontaneous Evolution. Our Positive Future. Hay House, 2011.

Dr. Bruce Lipton: The Biology of Belief. Hay House, 2015.

Esther and Jerry Hicks: Ask and it is Given. Learning to Manifest Your Desires. Hay House, 2007.

Evette Rose: Metaphysical Anatomy: Your Body is Talking, Are You Listening? Evette Rose, 2012.

Inna Segal: The Secret Language of Your Body. Atria Paperback, 2010.

Dr. Joe Dispenza: Evolve your Brain. The Science of Changing Your Mind. HCI Books, 2007.

Dr. Joe Dispenza: Breaking the Habit of Being Yourself. Hay House, 2012.

Dr. Joe Dispenza: You are the Placebo. Making Your Mind Matter. Hay House, 2014.

Dr. Joe Dispenza: Becoming Supernatural. How Common People are Doing the Uncommon. Hay House, 2017.

Karl Dawson and Kate Marillat: Transform Your Beliefs, Transform Your Life. EFT Tapping using Matrix Reimprinting. Hay House, 2014.

Lynne McTaggart: The Field. The Quest for the Secret Force of the Universe. Element, 2003.

Lynne McTaggart: The Intention Experiment. Use Your Thoughts to Change the World. Harper, 2008.

Lynne McTaggart: The Power of Eight. Hay House, 2019

www.ingramcontent.com/pod-product-compliance
Ingram Content Group UK Ltd.
Pitfield, Milton Keynes, MK11 3LW, UK
UKHW040627120225
455006UK00001B/10